Readers are invited to view and download the worksheets from *Play to Win*.

The worksheets are available FREE online.

If you would like to download and print out any of the worksheets, please visit www.josseybass.com/go/lapiana

Thank you,
David La Piana

PLAY TO WIN

PLAY TO WIN

The Nonprofit Guide
to Competitive Strategy

David La Piana
with Michaela Hayes

JOSSEY-BASS
A Wiley Imprint
www.josseybass.com

Published by Jossey-Bass
A Wiley Imprint
989 Market Street, San Francisco, CA 94103-1741   www.josseybass.com

Jossey-Bass books and products are available through most bookstores. To contact Jossey-Bass directly,
call our Customer Care Department within the U.S. at 800-956-7739 or outside the U.S. at
317-572-3986, or fax to 317-572-4002.

Jossey-Bass also publishes its books in a variety of electronic formats. Some content that appears in print
may not be available in electronic books.

Library of Congress Cataloging-in-Publication Data
La Piana, David, date
  Play to win : The nonprofit guide to competitive strategy / David La Piana, with Michaela Hayes.
      p. cm. Includes bibliographical references and index.
  ISBN 0-7879-6813-7 (alk. paper)
1. Strategic planning. 2. Competition. 3. Organizational effectiveness. 4. Nonprofit
organizations. I. Hayes, Michaela. II. Title.
  HD30.28.L372 2005
  658.4'012—dc22   2004015132

Printed in the United States of America
FIRST EDITION
HB Printing 10 9 8 7 6 5 4 3 2 1

CONTENTS

PART THREE: DEVELOPING COMPETITIVE STRATEGIES   127

FIGURES, TABLES, EXHIBITS, AND WORKSHEETS

Figures

Tables

Exhibits

Worksheets

This book is lovingly dedicated to the memory of my father, Charlie La Piana.

PREFACE: WHY A BOOK ABOUT NONPROFIT COMPETITION?

This book is intended to strengthen nonprofit organizational effectiveness by helping leaders to make more effective use of competitive strategy. It makes the case that being a more effective competitor will enhance your nonprofit's chances for both programmatic and financial success, and it provides practical tools for assessing your nonprofit's position in the market and then developing competitive strategies that will improve your market position.

Competition can be defined as the process of different entities vying for an optimal share of a limited resource. This book emphasizes competition as an approach to securing the resources necessary for your nonprofit to advance its mission. Competitive strategy is the path to finding and securing the resources and opportunities most appropriate to your organization, based on its mission and expertise and in light of its comparative advantages in the market. *Competitive strategy* can be defined as a pattern of thoughtful action through which an organization's leaders seek an increased share of limited resources, with the goal of advancing their mission. If you are an experienced nonprofit competitor, this book will provide a framework for thinking about what you already do intuitively and for developing a fuller understanding of competitiveness. If you are coming to the concept of nonprofit competition for the first time, it will serve as a primer on the subject.

Competition in the Nonprofit Sector

Nonprofit leaders and their funders frequently discuss collaboration as a vehicle for improving both organizational effectiveness and program delivery. Competition is less frequently mentioned, but it is also a powerful dynamic and a commonly used means of achieving the sector's ends. In fact, competing successfully is necessary for survival and success.

Nonprofits compete—sometimes indirectly, sometimes more directly and intensely—on a variety of fronts, against business and government as well as against one another. Nonetheless, nonprofit leaders often find it uncomfortable to discuss or even to acknowledge the existence of competition, since the sector defines itself as inherently collaborative in nature.

For some nonprofit leaders, the very idea of competition conjures images of cigar-chomping capitalists who will do anything for a buck. For example, an article in *Association Management* asks, "Can the inherently collaborative philosophy of [nonprofit] 'association' co-exist with the predatory mind-set required for free-market, 'winner-take-all' competition?" (Houstle, 2003). I believe that competition is essential to the nonprofit sector and that a better understanding of competition and a fuller appreciation of its complexity and usefulness can help nonprofits to make better use of this important strategic tool.

Recent work sheds light on nonprofits' reluctance to respond competitively to competitive challenges. Hopkins and Hyde (2002) studied 115 human service managers, 40 percent of whom identified "competition for clients or funding" as a major challenge. This was by far the most frequently reported challenge in the study. However, when asked to identify responses to the challenges they had just named, 46 percent of respondents said "staff development," 44 percent identified "fundraising," and 40 percent indicated "staff recruitment." "Strategic planning," the next most popular response, was reported by only 27 percent of respondents. Searching for a response that might correspond to the competitive challenge that the managers interviewed for the study had themselves identified, we must go down the list to "marketing," which was reported by only 17 percent of respondents.

The managers in this study clearly see competition for resources as a major challenge, but nowhere in the list of strategies for responding to this challenge do they utter the word *competition*. The researchers lament: "It is distressing that there is little evidence that managers understand the import of visionary and innovative responses to these challenges. Often, solutions did not match with the identified challenges" (Hopkins and Hyde, 2002, p. 10).

Collaboration at least made the list; it was named by 14 percent of respondents. Competition did not. Clearly, when facing strategic challenges, competition can be the right tool for the job at least as often as collaboration. Given the nature of the challenges the managers in this study identified, either approach would be preferable to responses such as "staff development," because, at the very least, collaboration and competition both are concerned with conditions and relations in the environment external to an organization, which is where the "competition for clients and funding" that the managers are worried about comes from.

The disconnect between practice (nonprofits do in fact compete) and principles (nonprofits believe they are inherently collaborative) motivated the writing of this book, which advances a view of both competition and collaboration as necessary, appropriate, useful, and often intertwined paths. Specifically, this book addresses why and when to compete with others in your market and how to do so both effectively and ethically.

Ethical Competition

For some, the idea of competing for resources with other nonprofits seems at best suspect and at worst unethical. But competition can—indeed must—be ethical; strategic choices must be made within a larger context than simply what is best for a single nonprofit's bottom line (or for the career of its executive director). To be ethical, competition must be in pursuit of a social mission, never for self-aggrandizement, ego massage, or empire building. You are, after all, part of the mission-driven sector: you compete for resources in order to advance your social mission. The concept of ethical competition is integral to this book's case for competition as an essential part of nonprofit strategy.

Every nonprofit has competitors for resources of one kind or another; usually many different competitors for several kinds of resources. Ethical competition can be a powerful catalyst for growth. A mental health services nonprofit that I directed grew over several years from serving twenty children into a much more effective organization serving more than four thousand children. This growth was accomplished through a combined strategy: collaborating with others to execute three mergers while competing for grants, contracts, and public recognition based on our responsiveness and effectiveness. Our competitiveness helped us to serve many more families and to gain many kinds of resources from a variety of sources. It also forced us to continually improve our services as we created a more sustainable organization. The competitive path we took led to a reexamination of both our programmatic and financial structures. It resulted in a major shift from a professional staff orientation to one driven by and largely employing people from the communities we served. Thus, competition was a powerful agent for fundamental change within our organization as well as for social change affecting the community.

Your effort to gain a competitive advantage in a field or community begins with the acknowledgment that competition can be a powerful force to improve your organization's effectiveness; it requires taking a hard look at your organization's ability to get the job done. To compete ethically, you must be confident that your work is making a difference. Nonprofits that can deliver effective programming within a strong, accountable, and sustainable structure must win resources—and those resources will come largely at the expense of nonprofits that, despite all their efforts, have not been able to deliver. This declaration amounts to an ethical imperative for competition, and it is a touchstone that I will return to later in this book.

The Need for Collaboration and Competition

In recent years, collaboration has received a great deal of attention, and today it is far better understood in all its complexity. As an example of how much work has been done in this area, see the collaboration resource list that was compiled by Kirsten Nielsen (2003). Competition in the nonprofit sector is a different story; few resources exist on the topic. The best thinking to date on nonprofit competition is from Kevin Kearns (2000), whose work helped to inspire this book. In order to encourage more balance between the current flood of writing on collaboration and the relative dearth of new thinking on competition, I will emphasize the possibilities offered by competitive strategies while placing competition within a context large enough to also accommodate collaboration. The framework that emerges offers options for making the most of the full range of possibilities for relating to others in a market—different levels of intensity of both collaboration and competition.

A better understanding of the full range of relationships with others (both collaborative and competitive) will help your nonprofit to achieve its social mission. Nonprofit leaders talk a lot about collaboration. Indeed, many new initiatives are conceived as collaborative endeavors from the outset, because there is often an implied unity of interest or a hoped-for synergy within a community of nonprofits. (See my Web article "Real Collaboration: A Guide for Grantmakers" [La Piana, 2001] for a fuller treatment of this issue.) Reality can be at odds with this cooperative self-image, however. Within these same fields of endeavor, there is often, in addition to common interests, a great deal of impetus for competition—for funds, customers, staff members, volunteers, board members, media attention, and public recognition. In reality, just as in the business sector, nonprofit collaboration and competition exist as a spectrum of relationships, not as polar opposites and certainly not as mutually exclusive choices.

Constructive Competition

This book addresses how to engage in constructive, ethical competition—that is, how and where to compete so that the overall field, community, or sector is strengthened. This book also demonstrates how to use collaborative strategies for competitive ends. However, three caveats must be noted at this point; each will help you, the nonprofit leader considering competitive strategy for your organization, to stay on track.

Get Your House in Order

Keep in mind that simply adopting an overtly competitive stance toward other nonprofits is not the answer. While most—if not all—nonprofits are implicitly competitive, a great many are also culturally adverse to the concept of competition. These nonprofits can still be high-performance organizations, but the idea of competition grates against their values. Overt competitiveness is not necessary to their success. Meanwhile, we all know of nonprofits that attract far more attention and funds than they deserve. These organizations may be very competent competitors, but perhaps they are not such effective organizations when it comes to delivering a social benefit.

The first rule, then, is to get your house in order: to design and conduct valuable activities, programs, and services within a structure that is both defensible and sustainable. You must first come to understand the relative value of your programs and only compete to sustain or build those which have both value and a reasonable chance of success. This caveat is also just good management. Ultimately, a great competitor is still likely to fail if it is a mediocre performer.

Know Yourself

The second caveat is political and cultural. Kevin Kearns writes that a nonprofit must first determine whether it wants "to play the competitive game" (Kearns, 2000, p. 75). If the organization is philosophically opposed to competition, he argues, it should steer clear of the types of programs that require it. If you are ambivalent about or opposed to competition, first acknowledge all the competitive activities that you are already engaged in. Simply put, your organization has not achieved its current level of success without competing. Perhaps you are really opposed to certain competitive attitudes associated with unsavory business practices or to the connotations of the term itself. If, in the end, you decide that competition really is not for you, then you should indeed heed Kearns's warning, although it is hard to think of a field of nonprofit endeavor in which competition is not an imperative. It is an inherent part of a nonprofit leader's world.

Define Value Inclusively

Finally, many isolated, rural, or oppressed communities have worked for decades to develop their own nonprofits. Some of these have grown into highly effective enterprises, while others continue to struggle. It is too simple to conclude that weaker nonprofits from these communities are less effective at carrying out a useful social mission than mainstream nonprofits that have a longer history or that have been able to tap into resources from the economic mainstream. Ethnic, sexual orientation, rural, and language minority communities create nonprofits that serve a complex set of needs. These nonprofits are where an immigrant goes first to volunteer, then to work, in the journey to becoming an American. They are objects of pride, community centers, places of emotional or even physical safety, and political hubs. They often serve customers with few resources who, even among nonprofits, may not represent very attractive markets. If the nonprofits that serve them fail, there may be no one waiting to take their place; certainly, it would be difficult for a mainstream organization to offer all of the helpful and protective cultural supports that would be lost. Thus, it is important to take a holistic approach when considering your competitive strategy in regard to these organizations; they may offer more value than meets the outsider's eye.

How This Book Is Organized

This book is organized in three major sections. An introduction sets the stage by describing the peculiar economic context of the nonprofit sector. The book then moves from a discussion of collaborative and competitive dynamics (Part One), to offering tools and processes for assessing your competitive position (Part Two), to suggestions for specific competitive strategies for gaining customers, third-party payers, human resources, or media and public awareness (Part Three).

Part One, "Understanding Competition in the Nonprofit Sector," has three chapters. Chapter One discusses the inherent limitations of collaboration as a strategy. Chapter Two brings competition out of the closet. It defines and describes competition among nonprofits, presents the concept of competitive strategy, and deals with some of the practical, ethical, and political ramifications of competition in the sector. Chapter Three presents the Nonprofit Strategy Matrix and related tools for understanding competition as part of a matrix of strategic possibilities that include collaboration.

Part Two, "Assessing Your Competitive Position," offers practical tools for assessing your nonprofit's competitive strengths and weaknesses (Chapter Four) and for assessing your competitive advantages and disadvantages vis-à-vis other nonprofits (Chapter Five) and within an entire sector or market (Chapter Six).

Part Three, "Developing Competitive Strategies for your Organization," offers four chapters, each focusing on developing practical competitive strategies for a specific area of activity: customers (Chapter Seven), third-party payers (Chapter Eight), human resources (Chapter Nine), or media and public awareness (Chapter Ten).

The book concludes with some observations on future competitive trends.

Uses of This Book

This book is intended to help you to think and act strategically, which in turn should contribute to greater organizational effectiveness and sustainability. It will help capable nonprofits to win resources away from those that are not so capable, and it will help marginally effective nonprofits to examine their reason for existence and then either improve their performance or consider bowing out of the marketplace.

Many good resources help nonprofit leaders learn how to collaborate. Far fewer help them to become better competitors or to understand the web of relationships—some competitive, some cooperative, some hybrid—that is necessary for success. This book focuses on helping you to develop your nonprofit's unique competitive advantages and then to use competitive strategies to build your organization's capacity for mission advancement. It will lead you to think through a new strategic outlook that involves a more aggressive competitive stance in the market. You will also gain a deeper understanding of the economic underpinnings of nonprofit life. This appreciation for the economic circumstances of your nonprofit may allow you to make better decisions about growth, fundraising, board development, and a host of other critical topics.

Audience

The book directly addresses nonprofit executive directors. However, its message may also be of interest to board members, funders, consultants, and students of nonprofit management—anyone interested in helping nonprofits to form strategies that can propel them to success. Ultimately, it is intended to help nonprofits to find their place among the many groups inhabiting virtually every field of the sector's endeavor.

Glossary

The following terms, used in the text, have a somewhat specialized meaning. I will define them up front for ease of later reference.

Business model: The economic model in which a willing buyer pays a willing seller an agreed-upon sum for an agreed-upon service or product. Recognizing that a host of government subsidies modify this model in the business sector, it is still in fact the model for most small businesses and is still the theoretical model for American business.

Collaboration: A range of relatively informal working relationships between organizations. When it becomes more formal or integrative, collaboration crosses the line to *strategic restructuring* (see that entry).

Competitive advantage: This concept can be summed up as the answer to the question, "Why would a customer, board candidate, potential employee, or funder choose one nonprofit over another?" It is the strength of one group relative to others in its market.

Competitive strategy: A pattern of thoughtful action through which a nonprofit's leaders seek an increased share of limited resources, with the goal of advancing their mission.

Customers: The users of a nonprofit's programs or the constituents of its cause. They might be opera patrons, members of an environmental group, or clients of a mental health clinic. Sometimes they pay to participate in their programs, sometimes not. The term does not do justice to the range of beneficiaries, members, recipients, participants, constituents, and audiences that nonprofits serve. However, for ease of use, this single term will be used.

Market focus: A nonprofit's market focus can be defined as a combination of the geographic area in which it works, the types of customers or constituents it serves, and the types of programs that it provides for their benefit. It defines the playing field on which you compete with others for resources.

Market share: The proportion of the total possible market that an organization can claim as customers.

Mission: The improvement or change a nonprofit seeks to achieve in the world.

Nonprofit economic model: A common economic model in which customers pay less than the cost of the benefit they receive. The resulting gap is covered by third-party payers.

Organizational effectiveness: I will use the Grantmakers for Organizational Effectiveness (www.geofunders.org) definition: "the ability of an organization to fulfill its mission by measurably achieving its objectives through a blend of sound management, strong governance, and a persistent rededication to assessing and achieving results."

Strategic restructuring: A range of partnerships among nonprofits that go beyond collaboration—for example, joint ventures, alliances, and mergers.

Strategy: There are many definitions of strategy. Here is a simple but useful one: a pattern of behavior that constitutes a way of moving an organization toward its goals.

Third-party payers: Funders that do not receive a direct benefit in return for their payment. Instead, they support the activities on behalf of the nonprofit's customers, either specifically (for example, through government contracts), or generally (for example, through a foundation general operating support grant). Funds from third-party payers include government contract payments, foundations or corporate grants, insurance reimbursements, and individual donations or bequests.

ACKNOWLEDGMENTS

I initially conceived of this book as an exploration of competition largely from an economic perspective—how the dynamics of the marketplace impel nonprofits to compete. As the project developed, however, it became clear that the book would be far more useful if it also contained practical advice on assessing an organization's competitive position and, further, what to do about it. In order to accomplish this expanded objective, I enlisted the help of Michaela Hayes, senior manager and director of marketing, research, and development for La Piana Associates, Inc. She brought to Parts Two and Three her vast knowledge and experience with marketing, market research, and communications strategies. Whatever is helpful in those parts is largely Michaela's doing.

Furthermore, Michaela and Liza Culick, another senior manager at La Piana Associates, and Heather Gowdy, a longtime senior associate, each read an early draft of this book and provided much useful (if sometimes painful!) feedback. Natasha Terk, another associate, slogged through numerous reference works in search of both new insights and citations of works used, and Kristen Godard, also an associate, did research for the literature review. Associate Melicia Charles checked facts and ran down references for the final edit. These people and the rest of the La Piana Associates team consistently inspire me and one another to do the very best we are capable of in all our undertakings.

When Johanna Vondeling originally approached me about writing this book, I had only the vaguest idea of where the project would go. Over the ensuing year and a half, she provided key guidance at critical times and support and encouragement throughout. I am deeply in her debt.

For many years, I have been interested in the question of how nonprofits can make more effective use of strategic thinking in advancing their missions. From the vast literature on strategy, mostly written for a business audience, Henry Mintzberg's work has always struck me as most intriguing. His deep and novel insights, general irreverence, and sheer writing verve have inspired me to think beyond the tried and true (but not always helpful) confines of strategic planning.

In the course of researching this book, I had the opportunity to interview Mintzberg, as well as several other notable thinkers whose work I admire. In the first rank stands Kevin Kearns, whose *Private Sector Strategies for Social Sector Success* should be required reading for every student of nonprofit management. In addition, Jim Phills of Stanford University Graduate School of Business; Paul Light of New York University and the Brookings Institution; Don Watters, a partner at McKinsey & Company and longtime colleague; Katherine Fulton of the Monitor Institute; Ian MacMillan of Columbia University Business School; and Mark Kramer of Foundation Strategy Group gave generous interviews that greatly complicated—and enhanced—my thinking.

I want to acknowledge my wonderful family—Mary McFarland, my wife of twenty-five years, and my daughters, Marisa and Tessa—and publicly ask their forgiveness for all the time I stole from weekends, nights, and "vacations" to complete this work. Finally, this book is dedicated to my father. Just weeks before its completion, he died, at age eighty-nine. We all miss him, but no one more than my mother, Jean La Piana, who remains my great friend and most ardent supporter.

D.L.

THE AUTHORS

David La Piana is founder and president of La Piana Associates, Inc., a consulting firm specializing in strategic issues for foundations and nonprofit organizations nationwide. He has been an adjunct professor at the University of San Francisco's Institute for Nonprofit Organization Management and a lecturer at the Haas School of Business at the University of California, Berkeley. Recognized as an expert on strategy and partnerships among nonprofit organizations, David has worked extensively with funders and nonprofits in health, human services, the environment, and the arts, and he coined the term *strategic restructuring*, referring to a range of nonprofit partnerships.

A nationally popular speaker and teacher, David is the author of *The Nonprofit Mergers Workbook: Part II* (with the La Piana Associates team, 2004), *Nonprofit Strategic Restructuring: Mergers, Integrations, and Alliances* (with Amelia Kohm, 2003), *The Supplemental Assessment Tool for Start-Ups* (2003), *In Search of Strategic Solutions* (2003), *Real Collaboration* (2001), *The Nonprofit Mergers Workbook* (2000), *Beyond Collaboration: Strategic Restructuring of Nonprofit Organizations* (1997), and *Nonprofit Mergers* (1994), as well as numerous articles and opinion pieces on nonprofit boards, strategy, and executive leadership.

Since 1979, David has worked as a nonprofit staff member, executive director, trainer, consultant, and board member. A former VISTA volunteer, he has held leadership positions with the YMCA of San Francisco, The International

Institute, and East Bay Agency for Children, a multifaceted human services agency that grew tenfold under his leadership.

David received undergraduate and graduate degrees in comparative literature from the University of California, Berkeley, and a master's degree in public administration from the University of San Francisco's Institute for Nonprofit Organization Management. He has also studied at the University of California, San Diego, and at the Universidad de Madrid in Spain. He is a Salzburg Seminar Fellow and has received recognition for his work in the nonprofit sector from the mayor of Oakland and the California state assembly. He lives in Piedmont, California, with his wife, Mary McFarland, and his children, Marisa and Tessa.

Michaela Hayes is a senior manager with La Piana Associates, where she specializes in research and development, and marketing and communications. She has an extensive background in population, market, and survey research; marketing; communications; strategic planning; and program development and evaluation. Michaela has held manager and director-level positions in marketing and market research with several organizations, as well as senior and managing consultant positions with national consulting firms.

Michaela's professional work spans the nonprofit, for-profit, and government sectors, and includes organizations focused on health care, mental health, social services, children and youth, seniors, environment, education, and arts and culture. She has designed and conducted many research projects on behalf of clients who seek to better understand their markets and market trends, market position, competition, and customer-client needs. She advises clients on how to use market information to make better decisions and to develop more effective strategies to achieve their missions, as well as helping them to develop their own in-house research and marketing functions.

Michaela is a nonprofit board member and volunteer. She is active in the American Marketing Association, and serves on the board of the San Francisco chapter of the International Association of Business Communicators and on the Steering Committee of the Philanthropic Consultants Network. Additionally, she teaches in San Francisco State University's Integrated Marketing Program.

Michaela received a master's degree from the School of Public Health at the University of Michigan, and a B.A. degree from the University of California, Berkeley.

PART ONE

UNDERSTANDING COMPETITION IN THE NONPROFIT SECTOR

The goal of this Introduction is to furnish a context for the entire book by providing a working background on the economic and psychological dynamics that shape competition in the nonprofit sector. An enormously complex topic, it will be presented in a brief and practical format that focuses on key concepts.

I begin with the concept of market failure, exploring the critical role of third-party payers in the nonprofit economic model. I then review the psychological mind-set regarding interorganizational relationships that dominates the sector and urges its leaders toward collaboration as a response to market failure, whether or not that is the best choice in a given nonprofit's situation. As an alternative to collaboration, I will offer the concept of a competitive imperative, exploring the challenge it presents for the sector's leaders.

Competitive Strategy and Organizational Effectiveness

Our world needs strong, adaptable, effective nonprofits capable of formulating and then advancing powerful social missions. In order to become or remain such a nonprofit, you need to use all available tools—including competitive strategy. Ultimately, organizational effectiveness is about current and future accomplishments, and your nonprofit will get to its preferred future through the strategic decisions you and your staff and board colleagues make. Leaders of an effective nonprofit know, can find out, or at least have a hunch about what they need to do to succeed; competitive strategy is how they go about getting there.

Competitive strategy is concerned with determining how your organization will act on challenges that emerge from the environment. Strategic planning as commonly practiced in the nonprofit sector most often focuses on fine-tuning current efforts, not on identifying and responding to truly strategic, novel, or unpredictable challenges in the future. Since the future is innately unknowable, nonprofit strategic planning tends to focus more narrowly and more internally than it should, rather than more broadly on competitive threats and opportunities in the external world. Recent research suggests that "leadership has shifted from a mission-centered focus to a resource-driven focus, and that leadership is internally oriented, with comparatively little attention paid to the external environment" (Hopkins and Hyde, 2002). In order to succeed—to be an effective organization—your nonprofit must understand and improve its position in the external environment. We turn now to a look at that world.

The Economic Context: Market Failure

Market failure is the most basic economic rationale for the existence of the nonprofit sector. When a necessary activity is unlikely to generate a profit, the need must be addressed by people whose motivation is not, in fact, to generate a profit. As a result, many nonprofits operate within a unique economic context, one that fundamentally differs from that of the business world. They undertake programs that are unavailable from business either because the customers have little money (for example, homeless people); because the activity is so expensive that few people of any means could afford it without subsidy (for example, staging an opera); or because the activity, important as it is, does not have identifiable individuals as customers (for example, environmental advocacy). In each case, the business economic model does not work: while the need for a nonprofit's programs may be great, even overwhelming, it is simply not possible to undertake these activities as a service to a paying customer whose payment covers the nonprofit's cost, let alone allows for a profit. This situation turns on its head the business entrepreneur's constant search for market position with potential customers who can be provided with a desired product or service at a profitable price. In a typical nonprofit's experience, this becomes a search for resources to support delivery of a valuable but unprofitable program.

Market failure is not by any means limited to human services, where we commonly think of nonprofits providing services for impoverished customers who cannot afford to pay for them. If you are in the performing arts, you know only too well that ticket sales cover only a fraction of the cost of a major stage production. If you are in a low-income housing development, it is likely that tenants' rent does not meet the cost of the units they occupy and the on-site services they receive. If you provide legal aid services, your client pays little or nothing for legal representation that would cost thousands or even tens of thousands of dollars if it were being purchased.

This situation, of course, is not universal across the sector. Some nonprofits do indeed operate in a market economy that is similar or identical to the traditional business model. Moreover, the advent of certain third-party payers—such as managed care companies—has brought increasing competition from businesses intent on entering markets, such as health and human services for the poor, that until recently were almost exclusively the domain of the public and nonprofit sectors. At the same time, nonprofits are increasingly developing their own business enterprises, which range from mission-related job training programs to purely commercial undertakings such as opening a franchise of Ben and Jerry's. Although entrepreneurial activity among nonprofits is at an all-time high, for most nonprofits customer payments fall far short of the cost of providing services, no matter how efficient the organization may be.

The line between what businesses do and what nonprofits do has never been more blurred. One thing, however, is unlikely to change: nonprofits still dominate the market for activities that do not generate a profit.

Consider your own nonprofit. Do your customers (your constituents or end users, however you define them) pay for the activities that your organization undertakes on their behalf? How much of your actual costs do they pay for? A small amount? Half? Nearly all? Keep your answer to this question in mind as you read on.

You may well accept that nonprofits exist in a different economic context from business. But you might also wonder just how market failure affects nonprofit economics. You know that, unlike most businesses, nonprofits often do not receive all, or in some cases any significant portion, of their revenues from the beneficiaries of their activities. They need other income sources. For many nonprofits, third-party payers—government, private insurers, philanthropic foundations, corporations, and individual donors—are absolutely essential to the revenue mix. It is the presence of these third-party payers—particularly, in some fields, where government plays a central role—that, as a result of market failure, so deeply affects the nonprofit economic picture. Let's first take a brief look at the role of government in the nonprofit economy, then turn to the topic of third-party payers itself.

The Role of Government

Government is often described as the "safety net" service provider, and, indeed, responsibility for various essential services falls principally to local government. However, since the dawn of the Great Society in the 1960s, government at all levels has increasingly contracted with nonprofits for the provision of many of these services. Since the move toward block grants, devolution, and local control that began in earnest in the 1980s with the Reagan Revolution, government has increasingly turned to contracting out these services in order to reduce costs and make use of the nonprofits' closer ties to the communities served (Salamon, 1989).

The reasoning behind this outsourcing model was famously described by E. S. Savas and quoted by Osborne and Gaebler (1993) at the outset of their influential book *Reinventing Government*: "The job of government is to steer, not to row the boat. Delivering services is rowing, and government is not very good at rowing." Over time, however, nonprofits' costs for rowing the government's boat have steadily grown, while for the nonprofit oarsmen, cost-of-living increases in government contracts have fallen well behind the true cost of doing business. This growing gap has necessitated a shift in the role of nonprofits as government contractors: increasingly, they now see themselves as partners with government, generating a substantial proportion of their own revenues in support of publicly sponsored or mandated programs (Smith, 1994).

Nonprofits fill a need that the government has decided (through its funding levels, reimbursement rates, and other fiscal and contracting policies) will not be filled for profit. Nonprofits are willing to fill these needs, but not because they see themselves as agents of government. On the contrary, nonprofits tend to view government as a funding source that helps them to carry out their own missions, which are inevitably larger than the aims of any government contract.

Throughout the economy, the failure of markets to attract businesses to crucial activities, coupled with government's well-founded reluctance to directly provide a host of services that it is nonetheless mandated to take responsibility for, creates an opportunity for nonprofits to expand their work in these fields, not merely as agents of government but as a vital link in the chain of interdependence that constitutes our civil society. Remember, the people who work in nonprofits do so not in order to carry out a legal mandate (like government) and not in order to generate a profit (like business); they do their work quite simply to advance a cause they believe in with all their heart (Light, 2002a). (Now, *that* is a competitive advantage!)

Government funding opportunities also create competition within the sector, since government contracts, with all their complexities and entanglements, are often reliable, renewable sources of funds and are thus highly prized among different nonprofits vying for resources in the same field.

Third-Party Payers

The curious thing about third-party payers is that they do not receive a direct benefit from the activity they support; they purchase it on another's behalf, and the benefit they are purchasing accrues to someone else. Government, of course, is required by various laws to support certain activities. Philanthropy, however, is voluntary. While it is essential to our civil society and often represents human nature at its best, philanthropy makes little sense from an economic perspective, where a person can be expected to act first and foremost out of economic self-interest.

Nonetheless, the fact that people and institutions do in fact act philanthropically provides further evidence that nonprofits operate in a different economic context from business. Third-party payers have a mix of political, legal, commercial, and philanthropic motivations, as well as, quite often, a big dose of personal, values-driven interests. As a result, it is not that basic economic principles do not apply to nonprofits, but rather that there are additional principles, derived from their missions and from the motivations of their supporters, which further complicate the picture, making the role of third-party payers central, complex, and critical to nonprofits' competitive success.

Added to the unpredictable mix of third-party payers are client or user fees and investment income, for those nonprofits fortunate enough to have either; the proceeds from any earned income ventures; and funds from participation in federated campaigns. Taking it all together, a nonprofit's revenue stream might be more aptly viewed as a dense, nearly impenetrable swamp consisting of eddies, springs, quicksand, and an occasional waterfall. Thus, it is clear that the necessity of third-party payers greatly complicates the sector's finances, and, as we shall see, the nonprofit leader's competitive motivations.

Nonprofits that are heavily supported by third parties must consider the needs and demands of their funders in all planning and decision making. If not, other competitors are waiting to move in. Given this reality, there is a great temptation to serve the priorities of third-party payers, who in essence can become the organization's primary constituents, replacing customers as the nonprofit's most important consideration when it comes to decision making. This phenomenon is well captured in a *Nonprofit Quarterly* article by McCambridge and Salamon (2003, p. 11): "[The nonprofit economic model] . . . creates a class of nonprofit 'stakeholders' whose impact on nonprofit organizations can easily exceed that of the organization's 'customers.'" This dual allegiance can confuse even the most well-intentioned of nonprofit leaders, who may occasionally forget whom their organization is ultimately intended to serve.

McCambridge and Salamon go on to describe a situation in which the expressed priorities of homeless people and those of the funders of homeless services differed: "Because of the power dynamics between funders and nonprofits, the funders' frames of reference carry more weight. The views of the homeless people using the programs barely registered" (p. 14). In the long run, however, the needs of customers, as they define those needs for themselves, will be essential to your success, so don't let pressure from third-party payers crowd them out of your consideration.

The power of third-party payers is often invisible to the public and especially to a nonprofit's customers, but it is nonetheless real. As a result of the pressure to find and keep third-party payers, nonprofit leaders, particularly those with pressing financial needs, will be tempted down a dangerous path known as "mission creep."

Mission Creep

Mission creep is the pernicious process of moving further and further away from your nonprofit's core mission. When it is taken to an extreme, fundraising can become an organization's primary focus. It begins innocently enough when a potential new third-party funding source appears. The problem arises when the new pot of money turns out to be intended for activities that are only tangentially related to the organization's mission. Every leader faces borderline choices from time to time. A new opportunity may be tangential, or it may represent a maturation of the field or even the beginning of a true, strategically motivated shift in mission. Changes in direction are not always evidence of mission creep.

However, for the nonprofit experiencing an extreme form of mission creep (and there are many), the mission statement can be rewritten in one word: survival. When the search for funding replaces your social mission as the primary concern of your nonprofit enterprise, new opportunities are screened primarily for their likelihood to successfully garner resources, not for the appropriateness of the activity to your mission and competencies. If you reach this point, your organization has lost its moral rudder and is primarily concerned with its own survival and financial stability. This is not a strong competitive position from which to plot a future course for your organization but rather a directionless and dangerous meandering into uncharted waters. To compete successfully, you need a defensible set of programmatic activities that advance a coherent mission consistently over time.

One way to explain mission creep is that third-party payers have become the nonprofit's principal constituents, displacing its customers from that central role. Thus, the search for new opportunities and the decision about which to pursue are primarily focused on the availability of funding rather than on customer needs. This is a gradual, largely unconscious process. It usually occurs when you discover that your current mix of programmatic activities is essentially not competitive in the marketplace—that is, the program is unable to attract the support it needs to continue to be offered—but you are unable or unwilling to make the needed adjustments in either your programmatic or financial models. If you are tempted by a new, tangential activity, ask yourself, "If I didn't need the money, would this be as appealing?" An honest answer will start you down the road to the right decision. Part Two offers tools that you may find useful in deciding what market you are in and thus whether an opportunity should be pursued.

The failure of the market, which necessitates the intercession of third-party payers, resulting in confusion over who is your primary constituent, and the concomitant risk of mission creep, are all part of a complex economic picture that we can call the nonprofit economic model.

The Nonprofit Economic Model

Because nonprofits often occupy an economic no man's land in which they offer programs for one group (customers) but receive significant funding for those programs from another (third-party payers), it can be said that they are to some degree free of the discipline of the market, an imperative that causes businesses to conform their offerings to the expressed needs of identified, paying customers who are also their service users. Unlike freedom of speech, however, freedom from market discipline is not such a good thing, as we shall see.

A car dealer sells Fords to drivers; a silicon fabricator sells chips to computer makers; H&R Block sells tax return preparation to harried taxpayers; and a defense contractor sells tanks to the U.S. Army, and all of these customers pay for what they buy. Moreover, each of these customers pays enough to cover the provider's direct costs in delivering a Ford, a chip, a tax return, or a tank, plus enough to cover a portion of the provider's indirect costs for research and development, marketing, equipment depreciation, and staff training. On top of that, the customer pays enough to provide a profit for the business's shareholders. All of this is worked out in mathematical detail in the business world, where gross and net margins are calculated on every product or service. If the numbers don't support an activity, it is unlikely to be undertaken.

The usual nonprofit picture is quite different. In the nonprofit economic model, the customer either pays nothing or, using a sliding scale, pays less than full value for a program that a nonprofit and its third-party payers subsidize. Payment is often based less on the value provided than on the customer's ability or willingness to pay. Some art lovers would be able but most would be unwilling to pay $500 each time they entered a museum; most music lovers would refuse to pay $3,000 to attend a symphony concert; few parents could afford $75,000 for a year of residential treatment for their emotionally troubled child; and most environmental activists would blanch at the prospect of donating $100,000 toward the purchase of an endangered tract of land. Yet these might be the actual costs that the respective nonprofits incur for these activities that their customers desire, need, and depend on.

When I was executive director of a children's mental health agency, our treasurer, a bright young Stanford MBA, reviewed our year-end financial statement and noted that the line item "Client Fees" totaled a few hundred dollars, collected from our four thousand young customers. She commented with unmistakable irony: "This is truly a great business you're running here, David!" Similarly, your nonprofit might offer theater for kids but get paid by local government, though usually not enough to cover even the direct costs associated with the activity, let alone an allowance for research and development, marketing, staff training, depreciation, or accumulating a surplus. To make ends meet, you are forced to seek additional funds from foundation grants, corporate gifts, and individual donors. Sadly, your board may also subsidize the activity by paying substandard wages to you and your workforce, an often necessary but unfortunate practice.

Figure I.1 portrays the traditional business model, in which a customer's payment covers the provider's cost, plus profit, and the nonprofit economic model,

FIGURE I.1. THE TRADITIONAL BUSINESS MODEL AND THE NONPROFIT ECONOMIC MODEL.

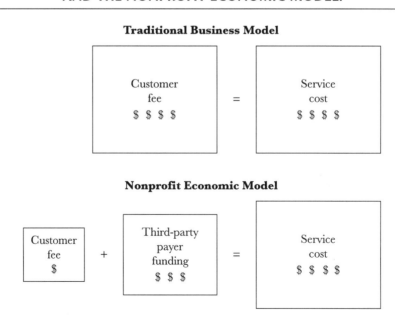

where it often does not, necessitating the intervention of third-party payers. This model was first developed by Hank Rosso in his seminars in the 1970s. In the nonprofit economy, third-party payers fill this gap because they want to see the activity undertaken.

Sometimes the third-party payer has a legal responsibility to do so, as in the case of local government contracts with nonprofits for mandated safety net services or the congressional allocation for the quasi-public National Endowment for the Arts. Other third-party payers have a philanthropic interest in advancing a particular cause, as in the case of philanthropic foundation grants that support selected nonprofits in their fields of interest. Still other third-party payers act out of a mixture of philanthropic intent and self-interest—for example, in the common practice of corporate sponsorships of charities.

The distinction between these models has profound consequences for competitive concerns in the two sectors. Businesses know that their ability to identify, cultivate, and satisfy paying customers is key to success. Thus, their competitive strategies are aimed at clearly demonstrating to current and potential customers that their offerings are superior in some ways to those of their competitors. For nonprofits, the fact that their customers and their payers are, to varying degrees, different people can confuse their efforts to meet the needs of each.

In this complex world of mixed motivations, faced with an ever-present need to fuel the enterprise with new funds, ideas, supporters, and staff and board members, you can be forgiven for occasionally having to think twice about whether your primary customer is the person in need or the person with the money to pay for meeting that need. This question arises because of the lack of immediate, direct, life-or-death market feedback, something that the business leader can often count on but that you must go out of your way to secure. Remember, as I said earlier, freedom from the discipline of the market is not a good thing. For example, it does not help you to see competitive threats that may arise from others who are rapidly becoming better able to meet the needs of your customers.

The nonprofit economic model provides an enormously complex situation for you to manage. You can see this phenomenon at its most pernicious when a customer needs ongoing care to recover from a severe depression, but the government contract that pays for the service stipulates a limited timeframe for treatment, or when a major donor to a museum tries to influence the choice of shows, themes, or interpretations. More innocently, you also see it at work every day when your customers want a higher volume of service, but your board and your own good judgment tell you that you cannot afford to provide any more.

These difficult situations are often present in the nonprofit economic model, although you may not identify them as being caused in large part by the central economic role and power of the third-party payer, and, further, you may not see the

FIGURE I.2. NEEDS OF CUSTOMERS AND PAYERS IN THE BUSINESS AND NONPROFIT MODELS.

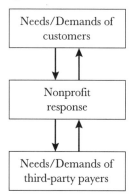

impact that these situations can have on your competitive position. However, viewing them in this light can help you to at least identify the root cause of the challenge you face and, hopefully, begin to find an answer. Figure I.2 portrays the simplicity of the business model feedback loop as compared with the nonprofit economic model.

The split between the needs of third-party payers and those of customers is made more pronounced and more problematic by the fact that you usually have a pretty good sense of what your third-party payers expect from you—either through contract language, grant award letters, or a donor's restrictions accompanying a gift—while you may have a much sketchier sense of your customers' needs. Third-party payers, by virtue of the fact that they are giving you money, are likely to be fairly explicit in stating what they expect in return. In contrast, your customers must be asked about their needs in ways that elicit honest and reliable answers. Given the greater weight that human nature is likely to attach to the needs and demands of someone offering something (money) as opposed to someone asking for something (a service), there is a natural tendency to put third-party payers' needs and demands ahead of those of customers. This must be countered by ongoing attempts to find out what customers think and need. Chapter Four provides some tools for doing this.

In order to be a competent competitor, for both customers and the resources to serve them, you must understand the nonprofit economic model, especially the role and influence of third-party payers. Moreover, your ability to stay focused on your mission and to avoid mission creep depends on your ability to remain psychologically independent of your major third-party payers, despite their critical role in your success. This last point moves us from the economic context within which nonprofits operate to a consideration of the psychological context within which nonprofit leaders live.

The Psychological Context: "Let's Collaborate"

The economic circumstances just described exist within a psychological environment in which nonprofit staff members are highly dedicated both to their work and to their organizations and are motivated by a desire to effect social change (Light, 2002a). Whatever the field of endeavor, people are drawn to nonprofit work by a desire to make the world better, to remake it to some degree along lines they would prefer—a place of greater justice, fuller equality, peaceful co-existence, and so forth. This motivation leads us to an ethos of collaboration. After all, we all want the same thing, don't we?

Nonprofit leaders and funders frequently talk of making a place at the table for the many nonprofits in their community concerned with a particular need. This thinking leads to collaboration as a mechanism for spreading limited resources across many nonprofits. Each group undoubtedly cares deeply about the issue at hand but, by its very participation, may dilute the funds available for mission-related program activities while bringing to the table relatively little of unique value. This approach also adds a cumbersome collaborative layer to any operation, which further drains resources from the mission-related work of all participants. All this, of course, is done in the name of enhanced synergies among nonprofits working on the same problem, so it is hard to argue against. Does this situation sound familiar?

Collaborating can be very difficult indeed, but it is what third-party payers often want. Be aware that when, either on your own or bowing to funder pressure, you focus primarily on working collaboratively with others in the same field or community to the exclusion of competitive strategies, you are turning away from an attempt to concentrate resources in your own nonprofit. While collaboration might make sense in a given instance, a competitive strategy may be more appropriate if your nonprofit is highly effective in addressing a particular need.

A reliance on nonprofits' socially sanctioned we're-all-in-the-same-boat collaboration rhetoric, which often has little real cooperative intent behind it, and the unwillingness of third-party payers to acknowledge and support head-to-head competition among the nonprofits they fund, can lead you to form poor alliances and to miss opportunities in which you might be better able to address a social problem than others. When you are trapped in such a situation, you usually know it, but a combination of the factors just described may inhibit you from expressing such a view. In my consulting work, I often encounter nonprofit leaders who, because of third-party payer or nonprofit value pressures, are pursuing collaborative rather than competitive strategies while experiencing competitive rather than collaborative motivations.

Ian MacMillan (1983), in his seminal article on nonprofit competition, argues that nonprofits should identify programs in which they have a competitive advantage or where there is no one else to fill an essential need and then compete for resources in those areas. He also recommends considering the transfer of some programs to better-qualified or better-positioned nonprofits. In this view, having everyone at the table only dilutes everyone's efforts. MacMillan told me in an interview that he believes that as a result (in part) of this ethos of collaboration, resources do not always find their way to the most effective actors in a given field.

When collaboration rules, the ability to deliver results may become less important in determining who is included in a new project than the mere willingness to collaborate. Collaboration can become the most important factor in the decision making of third-party payers. In an extreme case of collaboration mania, a public funder once issued a request for proposals, then asked the nonprofits that submitted competing proposals, including my own, to collaborate in deciding which groups would be funded. Obviously, the award committee, composed of the various competitors, quickly and hopelessly deadlocked. Clearly, there are times when competition is a better choice and times when it is, in fact, an imperative.

The Competitive Imperative

Your first task as a leader considering your nonprofit's competitive stance is to take an honest look at the merits of your current activities. The basic questions you must continually answer include these:

- Where should we build on our strengths with further investment?
- Where should we redesign and improve our execution in order to raise quality?
- Where should we divest, transfer, or close in order to minimize loss or harm done?

To make this assessment, it is necessary to look beyond your proud accomplishments of the past, beyond your staff's professional preferences and your board's inclinations, beyond even your third-party payers' expressed needs. You must look to your market position relative to your competitors, and you must ask your customers. Again, the prevalence of third-party payers and their distorting impact on nonprofit decision making makes this essential. Part Two will help in your effort to assess your market position and how well you are meeting your customers' needs.

Not everyone who makes this assessment will be happy with what they find. As a management consultant, I have had the privilege of working with hundreds of very effective nonprofits in virtually every field of activity. I have also encountered a few nonprofits that, frankly, would be doing the sector and the world a favor by closing their doors for good. This consulting experience has only reinforced my belief in a competitive imperative for the sector: nonprofits need to compete, based on effectiveness, as well as to collaborate, based on shared purpose, in order for the community to receive the best possible outcomes from their efforts.

Since there are not enough resources to go around, this is an ethical as well as an organizational imperative. Of course, nonprofit competition must not use a cutthroat, ego-driven, take-no-prisoners approach but should be undertaken thoughtfully, with an eye toward creating the ultimate good for the community, assessing the widest ramifications of each action. MacMillan (1983, p. 77) writes: "The most important consideration is to ensure that these competitive strategies should be constructive rather than destructive. There is need enough for resources without having them wasted by destructive competition. So it is essential to compete in such a way that it becomes demonstrably obvious to supporting organizations that the agency is superior to its competitors and thus capture support from key supporters."

During sixteen years as executive director of a rapidly growing nonprofit, I came to believe that it is the responsibility of effective nonprofits—those that deliver effective programs, live up to contractual commitments, manage their resources prudently, and truly make a difference—to do everything in their power to attract the resources they need to continue and expand their work. This includes, when the opportunity arises, winning resources away from less effective nonprofits through an ethical yet aggressive strategy that differentiates them from the pack of those offering similar services. This competitive imperative is driven by my belief that the mission of any nonprofit is not to provide jobs for social reformers or a sinecure for the well-intentioned but inept manager but, rather, to effect change, advance the nonprofit's social mission, and in the end actually make the world, or at least a small part of it, a better place. The bottom line: those nonprofits that are able to deliver on their mission should be strengthened, while those that fail, despite efforts that might be very well-intentioned, should fall by the wayside.

Ultimately, customers, third-party payers, and policymakers may determine which nonprofits thrive and which fail, by granting or withdrawing their patronage or support. But the day of reckoning is usually a long time off for any individual nonprofit. On a day-to-day basis, meanwhile, every nonprofit is trying to attract the resources it needs, through collaborative or competitive strategies. From the outside, it can be next to impossible to distinguish the more effective from the less effective nonprofit, but within the boardroom and the executive director's office at least, there should be no illusions.

Jim Collins's (2001) research into long-term successful businesses leads him to conclude that "you must retain faith that you will prevail in the end and you must also confront the most brutal facts of your current reality." Nonprofits have no shortage of people with faith in their cause, but that faith is not always tied to a realistic appreciation of the organization's current reality. Leadership that can face the brutal facts about the present while maintaining optimism about the organization's future can make all the difference. Like so many other elements of your nonprofit's existence, it ultimately comes down to you, working with other organizational leaders, to ensure that your nonprofit rises to this challenge.

The Leadership Challenge

Let's face it: the social and economic forces arrayed against most nonprofits are formidable. In the face of intractable social problems, lack of access to capital, fickle funders, a hostile political environment, poor management training, and low pay, it is amazing that nonprofits survive at all, let alone succeed. Yet, of course, a great many do in fact succeed. Despite numerous difficulties, the barriers to entry into the nonprofit world are relatively low. In many subsectors, little capital, specific expertise, or even customer base is needed to start a new nonprofit. A determined person with passion, a couple of friends willing to serve on the initial board, and a kernel of an idea can incorporate and apply for IRS 501(c)(3) status on her own, using a do-it-yourself book or at most a few thousand dollars worth of legal help.

Low entry barriers constitute just one factor leading to a large and ever-increasing number of nonprofits vying for space in many areas of the nonprofit sector. The IRS estimates that in 1952 there were 32,000 nonreligious nonprofits in the country. Today, there are well over 1.3 million (National Center for Charitable Statistics, 2004). While some young nonprofits bring new energy and ideas to bear on chronic problems, many other nonprofits just fail. Still others continue to operate indefinitely, attracting just enough resources to remain in the game but failing to achieve their founders' dreams. To one degree or another, most nonprofits are limited, either by the quality of their ideas, the consistency of their programmatic execution, or a lack of adequate resources to roll out their successful programmatic pilots. These limitations mean that most nonprofits quite simply are not able to affect their chosen cause to the significant degree they would like. This insufficiency can be extremely frustrating to the mission-oriented nonprofit leader. In this environment, competitive strategy is essential to your critical tasks of innovation, execution, and attraction of resources, so it must be better understood. A solid grasp of effective competitive strategies will enhance your chances of success as well as your job satisfaction.

Generally, it is difficult for either customers or third-party payers to distinguish from afar whether your nonprofit provides real value. This brings us to the nonprofit leadership challenge: you must have a clear understanding of and commitment to your mission in order to determine effective programmatic and organizational strategies, and you must continually assess your progress toward implementation of those strategies. Fortunately, most nonprofit leaders are up to the task. As Paul Light says, you came into the sector intending to make the world a better place, not to earn a pile of money (Light, 2002a). As an intrinsically motivated leader, you need to regularly reconnect with the social mission that brought you into the nonprofit sector in the first place; that connection will enable you to continually rely on your mission as a moral compass.

Within a business context, it may be good enough (though far from desired) for an inept enterprise to languish, failing to develop effective products or high-quality services but attracting just enough resources to limp along. After all, this is preferable to widespread layoffs of employees and leaving one's few loyal customers without their accustomed, if half-baked, product or service. Besides, there is always hope of a management turnaround; a technological breakthrough; a lucrative, growing, previously unrecognized market segment; or an act of God that will reinvigorate the business.

As a nonprofit leader, you don't have quite so much latitude. Hanging on while providing ineffective programs, so that your employees can maintain their jobs and a few regular customers can be served in a suboptimal manner, is simply not good enough. Since the sector's collective bottom line is not economic, but programmatic—not the wealth you create but the lives you transform—the ineffective nonprofit is both failing to advance the cause it is dedicated to and taking up resources that other, more effective actors could make better use of. Your nonprofit can be, independently, either financially or morally bankrupt; it can also be both at once. On the other hand, it is possible for your nonprofit to succeed, both programmatically and organizationally, and to do so in a fashion that is ethically sound. It falls to you as a leader of one of our more than one million nonprofits to choose and pursue a course for success.

Conclusion

This was a necessarily brief overview of the economic and psychological forces that shape the nonprofit competitive landscape. The key concepts—that many nonprofits exist due to market failure; that third-party payers play a critical but problematic role in the nonprofit sector; that nonprofits tend to rely on collaborative strategies at the expense of competitive ones; and that your leadership role is crucial—will help you to navigate the remainder of Part One and beyond.

CHAPTER ONE

THE LIMITS OF COLLABORATION

The merits of collaboration have been well covered in the extensive and often excellent literature on the topic. In this chapter, after a brief review of the concept of collaboration and a consideration of how it rose to such importance in the nonprofit sector, I will discuss its limitations as a strategy, not to discount collaboration entirely but rather to show that it is not a panacea for the environmental and economic challenges that nonprofits face. Collaboration can indeed be powerful, but it is not the appropriate response to every challenge. Thus, it is important to understand its limits.

In *Collaboration: What Makes It Work,* Paul Mattessich, Marta Murray-Close, and Barbara Monsey (2001) write: "Collaboration is not always effective. It is not always appropriate. Sometimes it might even result in greater costs than independent efforts. However, it does offer a strategic tool of value in many situations. Some people would predict that its popularity will continue to rise."

What Is Collaboration?

Judging from the amount written on the subject, and the frequency with which it appears on conference agendas, collaboration is indeed a popular way for nonprofits to relate to one another. As this book's bibliography attests, it has received wide consideration, yet there is not agreement on what the term means or, more

EXHIBIT 1.1. WHAT IS COLLABORATION?

What They Did	What They Said About It
A group of nonprofits, funded by the same California county, came together annually to lobby against budget cuts.	"We formed a collaborative to defend human services in our community."
Three nonprofits outside of Pittsburgh decided to merge into one new entity.	"We decided that closer collaboration would enhance our missions."
Four nonprofits in Illinois responded to a foundation RFP with a single proposal.	"We formed a collaborative to carry out this project."
Five nonprofits in Arizona decided to create a subsidiary organization to jointly market and coordinate their services.	"We knew we had to collaborate on these administrative services in order to save money, provide a better continuum of services, and build our market."
A Florida private school made space available on its campus for another nonprofit to provide services to its students.	"We decided to collaborate in order to better serve the kids."

specifically, where to set its boundaries. Collaboration, like obscenity, is notoriously difficult to define, but everyone in the sector seems to know it when they see it. The term itself has evolved over time and is used differently by various authors. In the nonprofit world each of the situations shown in Exhibit 1.1 has been called *collaboration.*

Exhibit 1.1 illustrates some of the variety of ways that nonprofit leaders use the term *collaboration.* What these instances have in common is that they involve two or more nonprofits working in concert on a given problem. In *The Nimble Collaboration,* Karen Ray (2002) describes two types of collaborations: those that integrate services among the collaborating nonprofits and those that are intended to resolve complex community problems. Ray's distinction is useful; another way to describe it is that collaboration is either internally focused on the organizational needs of the nonprofits involved or externally focused on the programmatic needs of common constituents. Each of the examples given in Exhibit 1.1 demonstrates nonprofits working together either to strengthen their organizations or to address an external or community problem bigger than any one party could tackle on its own. Essentially, then, in the nonprofit sector, collaboration simply means working together, and such a broad concept finds a wide range of expression. Paul Mattessich and his colleagues (2001) define collaboration as "a mutually beneficial and well-defined relationship entered into by two or more organizations to achieve common goals. The relationship includes a commitment to mutual relationships and goals; a jointly developed structure and shared responsibility; mutual authority and accountability for success; and sharing of resources and rewards" (p. 4).

Funder Pressure to Collaborate

It is a safe bet that if you have led a nonprofit during the past twenty-five years, you have at least heard of and have probably experienced collaboration. Philanthropic foundations often urge collaborative proposals from prospective grantees. Public funders give extra points to proposals submitted by collaborative groups. Often both private and public funders simply require collaboration as a part of the prospective grantee's proposal. Collaboration has been so widely hailed by third-party payers that it seems almost impolite to speak of its limitations.

In some communities, the widespread practice of formal collaboration has led to multiple and overlapping collaborative arrangements. It is not uncommon for leading nonprofits to be involved in many collaboratives at once. The membership of each of these separate endeavors has a high degree of overlap. This phenomenon drove funders and community leaders in Oakland, California, some years ago to create a metacollaborative consisting of representatives of all of the city's major collaboratives, which were themselves a shifting group of alliances based largely on current grant-funded projects. This group was given the difficult task of coordinating the activities of all the separate collaboratives that had sprung up around specific projects in targeted communities across the city.

It has long been apparent that funder-generated incentives or mandates drive much of this collaboration, as opposed to a real, heartfelt need to work together as perceived by the nonprofit leaders themselves. This is collaboration primarily for the sake of grantseeking, and often there is no real collaborative impetus. This *pseudocollaboration* has become a major time sink for nonprofit leaders, but because it is largely driven by third-party payers, it is difficult for nonprofit leaders to openly discuss it. Let's look briefly at some of the developments of the past quarter century that have strengthened the call for collaboration.

Economic and Competitive Pressures to Collaborate

Why has collaboration received so much attention during what Peter Dobkin Hall (1994) calls the postliberal era, beginning with the Reagan presidency in 1980? Hall points to the Reagan budget cuts as the source of a decisive shift in the nonprofit sector. He recounts how the Reagan administration simultaneously reduced expenditures for human services and shifted the burden for their delivery to state and local government, which were assumed to be capable of doing the job better and cheaper. These block grants led cash-strapped municipalities and counties to pass the buck, increasing their already heavy reliance on low-cost alternatives to their own civil service workforce: nonprofits.

Hall argues that funding in the nonprofit sector moved, at first gradually, then after 1980 with full force, from being primarily donated (mostly charitable gifts) to being more or less commercial (mostly earned income, specifically from governmental contracts): "If the organizations comprising the nonprofit sector in 1980 bore little resemblance to traditional donative charitable entities, a variety of forces over the course of the next ten years pushed them even further from common stereotypes. Even organizations that had resembled traditional charities before the Reagan era were compelled by a combination of federal budget cuts, weakened tax incentives for giving, and economic uncertainties, to move away from dependence on donations and toward a variety of earned-income strategies" (Hall, 1994, p. 27).

Ironically, part of the reason for the increased emphasis on collaboration beginning in this period may in fact be—greater competition. As economic pressures on nonprofits intensified and as they adopted increasingly commercial responses to these pressures, they necessarily became more competitive. For most organizations, this was not a conscious move—far from it—but they did begin to adopt more businesslike strategies, to experiment with social purpose enterprises and unrelated businesses, and to develop a preoccupation with greater size and market share. Is it a coincidence that as these shifts were occurring, we began to see the widespread adoption of the business term *CEO,* replacing the time-honored nonprofit term *executive director*? Or that this phenomenon coincided with a period in which a heroic view of corporate CEOs made them into popular culture superstars? (Think of the period from the ascendancy of Lee Iacocca to the retirement of Jack Welch.)

The pursuit of government contracts as a primary revenue source for the first time drew many nonprofits into direct competition with one another, as well as with service provision units that were directly operated by local governments (for example, health clinics, child care centers and arts programs), which were trying to avoid outsourcing. The growing focus of funding decisions at the local government level made collisions of interests among nonprofits both inevitable and public. In a primarily donative economy, nonprofits might seek funds from the same foundations, corporations, and philanthropists, but the process was episodic and often confidential, masking its competitive aspect. The situation changed with the shift to a focus on government funding. The processes through which government agencies awarded contracts were necessarily public, making it inescapably clear to everyone involved that they were in direct, often head-to-head competition with one another.

Sector Growth and Competitive Pressures to Collaborate

The past quarter century has been a time of relentless growth of new nonprofits. At the same time, mature nonprofits and new meteoric risers have secured market niches and obtained the best government contracts, making it ever more difficult for most newcomers to break in. This situation is only made worse during tough economic times, when there are few new dollars to spread around. If a newer nonprofit cannot directly compete for funding with its older counterparts because the contracting market is relatively static or is even declining, collaboration offers another way to secure a seat at the table. For these newer nonprofits, extolling the virtues of collaboration is also a savvy political move: the more established nonprofits cannot reject collaboration without appearing self-serving to their third-party payers.

Between 1940 and 1989, the number of secular nonprofits in the United States grew almost eightyfold, from 12,500 to nearly one million. Compare this to the sevenfold growth of new business entities in the same period (Hall, 1994, p. 19). There is not much information on the nonprofit dissolution rate, but it is likely that there has been a steady increase in the net number of nonprofits in operation each year. As each new entity is formed, pressure on the resources of third-party payers increases. Many philanthropic foundations report increased requests for funds each year (Foundation Center, personal e-mail exchange with the author, April 2003).

While so many new nonprofits were entering the world, hungry for funds, many of the 481,000 nonprofits that had been formed during the decade from 1967 to 1977 (fueled by the growth of the human services subsector as a result of the ambitious Great Society programs championed by President Lyndon Johnson) were reaching a maturity level that allowed them to control larger shares of their markets and thus to achieve (finally) a measure of financial stability. The strength of these organizations makes it especially difficult for new nonprofits to break into many local markets.

To give you a better idea of the prevalence of these baby boomer nonprofits, which now control so much of the government contracting market, consider that in 1967, there were only 309,000 nonreligious nonprofits in the United States. That number increased by 155 percent in the next decade (Hall, 1994, p. 19). While all this prosocial activity is commendable, there is not, economically speaking, an infinite amount of room in the sector for the unending waves of new players to occupy. As the numbers of nonprofits increase, so, inevitably, do the competitive pressures that all nonprofits labor under.

The Belief Paradox

As funding becomes more competitive, both funders and nonprofits develop coping strategies. Foundations tend to see more proposals each year from nonprofits that, from their perspective, look alike. A funder of youth theater is likely to receive many proposals from nonprofits that essentially do the same thing: present dramas featuring young casts. This situation leads to something that I call the Belief Paradox. It goes like this: If there is one belief that all nonprofits share, it is that they are unique. Unfortunately, if there is one belief that all funders share, it is that all nonprofits are the same.

I use this bit of hyperbole to draw your attention to the fact that from your funders' perspective, you may not appear to be as unique as you may believe you are; rather, they may merely consider you to be isolated from other nonprofits in your community or field. Foundation program officers naturally wonder why the various groups asking for funds toward the same end don't work together. After all, they reason, they are often trying to accomplish more or less the same thing.

Third-party payers such as foundations and corporate giving programs regularly see proposals from nonprofits working in different but (at least theoretically) complementary ways; their review of these proposals often reveals nonprofits working in isolation from one another. A funder of community-building initiatives, for example, may encounter a plethora of nonprofits, each trying to address the community's problems through a particular functional approach (for example, drug treatment, youth recreation, home ownership, access to health care, education reform, micro-enterprise promotion, crime reduction, teen mentoring, employment training, community arts, community organizing, or pregnancy prevention). There are staggering numbers of particularized approaches to virtually every social issue, each based on an often vast research literature and represented by cadres of highly trained professionals who view the overarching social problem primarily from their own professional perspective.

Alternatively, funders may review several proposals from nonprofits asking for support to conduct more-or-less identical activities. Whether it is providing shelter for battered women, sponsoring a summer concert series, or renovating decaying homes, there are often numerous nonprofits working on the same aspect of a problem. This is particularly true in urban areas. While there may well be a need for more of any of these activities, the lack of coordination among grantseekers and, often, the lack of even an acknowledgment that there are others in the field troubles funders.

The ongoing growth of the sector will not stop, and some new nonprofits do in fact represent breakthroughs in their fields. But so long as competition for philanthropic grants and government contracts remains strong, nonprofits competing for limited dollars will continue to be pressured by third-party payers to collaborate with one another.

The Rational Response

The rational economic response to an overabundance of potential service providers, most of whom have little clout with funding decision makers, is for the third-party payers to pick and choose the best values; after all, it is a buyer's market. Moreover, sunshine laws and accountability concerns lead public funders to use open bidding processes to award contracts, an inherently competitive approach to selecting contractors that is intended to yield the best service at the best price. However, even within these open processes, there are political pressures to be inclusive, to give everyone a seat at the table, or to be seen as offering an opportunity for a wide range of nonprofits to participate in any funding program. Moreover, the multiply determined social problems that many public and private third-party payers are concerned about make coordinated approaches all the more appealing; they do make sense. A variety of problem-solving approaches almost demands a coordinated strategy among several organizations. Therefore, collaboration is a necessary, though difficult and inherently inefficient approach to the sector's work that has its place among the strategic options available to any nonprofit enterprise.

Thus persists the idea, despite nonprofit leaders' fervent beliefs otherwise, that individual nonprofits are not unique in their ability to address a particular issue. Third-party payers such as government and foundations are largely united in their belief that nonprofits working in similar arenas should collaborate.

The Nonprofit Response

Nonprofits develop their own coping strategies for a competitive environment. If you are being honest, most of you readers will admit that you would rather receive a larger grant on your own, with no requirement to coordinate your efforts with others. (I know *I* would.) You may believe that you can achieve more through your own people and programs, over which you have some measure of control, but you agree to collaborate because you need the resources and recognition that come with being part of a funded collaborative effort. Being a realist, you are often willing to accept smaller grants than you would like, along with the task of collaborating with others, rather than risk receiving nothing at all. The feelings of countless nonprofit leaders about funder-driven collaboration could be summed up in the words of one executive, whom I quoted in *Real Collaboration* (La Piana, 2001): "I hate going to these Collaborative meetings; they are just a waste of time. My organization could do all of this more easily, better, faster and cheaper than the ten members of the Collaborative, but we couldn't get funding to do it on our own."

The picture is not all negative, however, where collaboration is concerned. Any phenomenon this popular must have redeeming qualities. Let's take a brief look at some of them.

Advantages of Collaboration

The advantages of collaboration have been recounted in great detail elsewhere. It is enough to say here that they are most readily seen "on the ground" in increased coordination of services. A food pantry and a transitional housing complex for people who have recently become homeless serve the same population. People in need of these services might spend much of their day traveling from the housing complex to the pantry and then back to their apartment. If the two nonprofits work together, however, they can at least provide transportation for their shared customers, and perhaps, over time, they can locate their services closer to one another. Similarly, a theater company might use its rehearsal and performance space only eighty hours a month on average, while a dance company from the same community pays top dollar for space it sublets from a local auditorium. Working together, the dance company can pay a reasonable rent to use openings in the theater's schedule, providing revenue for the theater and achieving savings for itself.

These are examples, respectively, of externally and internally oriented collaboration, according to Karen Ray's formulation. The first example is intended to directly help the nonprofits' shared customers, while the second primarily improves the financial situation of the two performing arts groups. This is where collaboration shines.

Disadvantages of Collaboration

Despite the positive features of combined effort, the road to collaboration is almost always bumpy. Nonprofit leaders often have strong independent tendencies that can make working with others difficult. On one consulting assignment, I traveled to a rural community to meet with the half dozen leaders of the area's local history museums. We discussed the possibility of colocating the groups in a series of re-stored, custom-designed facilities to be built in a depressed but historic part of town, thereby attracting tourists and infusing badly needed cash into the local economy. To me, an outsider, it sounded like a great idea. The first thing that struck me upon meeting this group of executives was that despite the fact that there were only six of them doing similar work in a small community, most did not know one another. They rarely if ever spoke and had never before met as a group. They came because they were invited by their most important funder. They were polite. But they made it clear that they had no interest in further discussions of this potential collabora-tion, although each organization would have jumped at the chance to undertake a new facility on its own. The point of the story is that many nonprofit leaders prefer not to collaborate, despite the obvious (to me, anyway) advantages of doing so.

The specific disadvantages of collaboration can be summed up as: the time barrier, strange bedfellows, and the lowest common denominator. Let's consider each in turn.

The Time Barrier

In addition to the human-made barriers to collaboration, there are drawbacks in-herent in this approach to solving problems. First and foremost among these is the amount of time and energy it takes to nurture and maintain real, enduring col-laborative relationships. You probably find it sufficiently challenging to keep your own board members, volunteers, and staff on the same page, sharing values and a vision of where they are going, and these, of course, are people who all belong to the same organization. Sharing values and a vision across nonprofits, let alone operating jointly, requires a huge investment of time and energy. Given the limi-tations imposed by everyone's workload, this is time that could presumably be spent doing something else equally or perhaps even more useful. Thus, unless the collaboration you are so heavily invested in is very successful, you are likely to begin to feel you are wasting your most limited and valuable commodity—your time.

Strange Bedfellows

Another drawback of collaboration is that you cannot always choose your collab-orators. Local politics, funder behests, and other external determinants may group you with organizations for which you have little affection or that are incompatible with you in their approach to the work to be undertaken. For example, a nonprofit that mobilizes people to clean vacant lots and plant community gardens may be paired with a low-income housing developer serving the same neighborhood. The exigencies of each nonprofit's "industry" will almost guarantee tension between a grassroots group that relies on community volunteers and a nonprofit that employs a professional staff, carrying out its work with federal funding in a highly regulated field.

The Lowest Common Denominator

A final drawback of collaboration can occur when, usually through funder pressure, collaboration becomes the dominant mode for undertaking almost any venture in a community. I once met with a group of nonprofit leaders who operated women's shelters in the same western city. They said they wanted to create a psychiatric inpatient unit for abused women with severe mental health problems who were thus not suitable for any shelter's program. We discussed at some length the difficulties and expense of such an undertaking. Finally, there was a pause, then a sudden shift in the conversation's direction.

One of the executive directors offered, "What if we buy a van, fill it with used clothes the women could 'buy,' and take it around to each shelter." I was confused. How could the clothes van, which sounded like a good idea on its own merits, meet the need that the psychiatric unit was supposed to address? Soon the answer became clear: it wasn't intended to. These executives were simply looking for something—anything—they could do collaboratively. Their funders were demanding closer cooperation among the shelters, so they had brainstormed a list of things they could conceivably do together. When the first idea appeared too difficult and expensive, they shifted to the next one on their list. Their primary intent was not strategic or even programmatic. Strategically, it seemed to make no difference to them if they embarked on a new multimillion-dollar, high-risk joint venture or simply bought a van and collected used clothes for their clients. The intent was collaboration per se, in order to meet a funder demand.

In such an environment, as you can imagine, it is essentially impolite and therefore politically dangerous to openly compete with other nonprofits for resources. It is similarly impolite for a funder to require nonprofits to compete for funds. Collaboration is considered the only real solution. I have seen situations in which well-functioning, successful nonprofits, which would be capable of accomplishing a great deal if they had access to more resources, are forced to work with marginal performers. The collaboration slows them down, wastes resources, and ultimately undermines the success of the entire venture. Often in these instances, the community would be better served by concentrating resources in a smaller number of highly effective nonprofits that can get the job done and letting the marginal performers fall aside. But these decisions are often more political than practical.

The Outer Limits of Collaboration

In addition to the difficulties (both inherent and human-made) with achieving and sustaining successful collaboration, it also has intrinsic limits as a strategy. You have just seen how collaboration can disperse resources instead of concentrating them among the organizations most capable of performing. While collaboration can bring together nonprofits working on different aspects of similar internal (organizational) or external (community) problems, strengthening their combined response to those problems, it can also have the opposite effect, weakening the combined or overall response of a community to a given social problem. This happens when a single strong nonprofit or several organizations working in parallel but not collaboratively (perhaps even competitively) would have a better chance of success. It also happens when the effort to manage the collaborative process drains resources from the work the collaborative was formed to undertake. The latter scenario—coordination efforts taking significant resources away from direct efforts—happens more often than many third-party payers realize and is a major source of dissatisfaction with collaboration among nonprofit leaders.

Sometimes promoting a collaborative approach provides cover for third-party payers or political leaders who do not wish to be seen as excluding and thus alienating a valued or powerful constituency. Frequently, I have found a group of nonprofits trying desperately to work together, even though one or more parties are adding little to the effort and are even hindering the group's progress, but have been included because it would be unacceptably impolitic to exclude them. This use of collaboration to avoid making choices, passing judgments, or being seen as playing favorites is problematic in itself. It also highlights the limits of collaboration as a strategy. There are three general limitations, situations in which collaboration is not the best choice for problem solving:

When there are insufficient funds available to address a problem through collaboration. For example, if a foundation grant to one environmental group is adequate for it to have a good chance of making a noticeable positive impact on an endangered ecosystem, but instead the grant is divided among several nonprofits and they are asked to collaborate to achieve the same results, not only are the resulting grants going to be smaller, but some of the funds that could have been spent on programmatic efforts must now be devoted to coordinating the collaborative itself. Will the smaller grants still enable the grantees, working together, to achieve the overall desired impact? If not, collaboration is contraindicated.

When some collaborators are incapable of meeting their responsibilities or advancing the work of the collaboration. For example, when two advocacy groups wish to share a long-term office lease, but one is not financially sound and could potentially fail, leaving the other group responsible for the lease payment, or when all the homeless programs in a city are asked by the mayor to collaborate, but several are known to offer poor-quality care and so are shunned by most homeless people, collaboration is ill-advised.

When the problem is better addressed through competition, letting market forces determine who provides the service. For example, would it be better for all the mental health counseling centers in a community to develop a central intake process whereby they assign clients based on the availability of counselors at each clinic, or would it be preferable for each center to compete for clients by providing high-quality, affordable services? In the latter case, word-of-mouth referrals might lead customers to choose the best service provider. Collaboration, although it ensures an even and predictable flow of customers—and funds—to all participating clinics, may not be the best answer for customers themselves.

In each of these circumstances, it might be better for the organizations and the communities involved to pursue a noncollaborative strategy to address a given problem. Sometimes collaboration is simply not the right strategy.

Collaboration often offers real advantages "on the ground," where services are coordinated, but at a stiff price. Many times, the results of collaboration do not justify the effort; resources are dispersed and the need for collaborative coordination grows.

Conclusion

We have seen that collaboration among nonprofits is a popular choice often urged by third-party payers. We have also seen that, despite practical advantages on the ground, where multiply determined problems can benefit from coordinated approaches, collaboration is not always the best strategic choice. Collaboration is limited in several ways, including the time it takes to make it a success, the difficulty in unifying nonprofits that have disparate values or approaches, and the tendency to include collaborators who may add little to a project. We also have seen that collaboration has inherent limitations as a strategy. Let's look next at another set of strategic options that avoids these pitfalls: competition.

CHAPTER TWO

COMPETITION OUT OF THE CLOSET

This chapter will help you to gain a clearer understanding of nonprofit competition. I define and explain the concept, which is a natural, inevitable, and underappreciated tool in the nonprofit sector. I describe the elements of competitive strategy, discuss how and why nonprofits compete, and review the idea of competitive advantage. I explore the positive and potentially negative aspects of competition in the nonprofit world by comparing and contrasting it with competition in the business world. I also briefly review the political, ethical, and cultural complications of competition, offering an orientation to the kinds of challenges that attend a decision to become more overtly competitive.

Competition in the Nonprofit World

What is competition, and how does it play out in nonprofit life? Nonprofits do indeed compete, often implicitly, for customers, donors, grants, staff, board members, volunteers, media attention, public recognition, and a host of other scarce resources. They compete with other nonprofits, as well as with government bodies and, increasingly, with for-profit corporations encroaching on what has traditionally been nonprofit turf.

As we have seen, the ethos of the sector is one of collaboration, which can sometimes make discussion of competition uncomfortable. Nonetheless, if you are unwilling to compete, you will not last long in our highly competitive world; resources will not just walk in the door. Kearns writes: "Understand that competition is a fact of life. At some level your organization is competing with other organizations whether you want it to or not." (2000, p. 27).

Here are some examples of competitive situations that may not be labeled as such by nonprofits:

• The marketing department of a performing arts presenter advertises its new show, which will run for a month. Patrons who choose to buy a ticket to one of these performances will implicitly but necessarily be choosing not to attend events sponsored by other presenters on those same nights. Similarly, they will be choosing not to rent a video, attend a basketball game, go away for the weekend, or spend a quiet evening at home. They may have a limited budget for entertainment, which they are dipping into to buy a ticket. Time and money are limited resources, and choices are constantly made about how to invest them.

• A day care provider opens a new center located along the morning commute route, hoping that harried parents will see the convenient location, be attracted to the nice building, and decide to enroll their children. Since these customers are already purchasing child care from another provider (a for-profit, a nonprofit, a family member, or an in-home nanny), opening the new center in an attractive location is a blatantly competitive move. The operator of the new center may not think this way, but she is undeniably hoping to lure parents away from competitors—other providers—unless her strategy is to attract only families with new children or those who have just moved into town.

• An environmental advocacy group seeks a foundation grant to support its work in a threatened watershed. Since foundations have limited grants budgets, the nonprofit is implicitly hoping to win a grant at the expense of another environmental cause that must be turned down. The group might not see it this way. In fact, it is likely that the successful grantseeker knows of other nonprofits that are also applying to this foundation. Its leaders might regret the lack of resources to fund all worthy proposals to save the planet. Nonetheless, this regret usually stops short of a willingness to share the successful organization's grant funds with others.

Defining Competition

As I stated in the Preface, competition is, in its essence, simply the process of different entities vying for an optimal share of a limited resource. In the earlier examples, the limited resources included free time and available funds for attending cultural events; children to place in child care and funds to pay for it; and grant dollars to invest in worthy environmental causes. Whenever there is an inadequate supply of something to meet the expressed need for it, you have a naturally competitive situation.

Competitive Strategy

In the Preface I defined *competitive strategy* as a pattern of thoughtful action through which an organization's leaders seek an increased share of limited resources, with the goal of advancing their mission. The process of adopting a competitive strategy may involve projections or forecasting and the establishment of specific multiyear goals, a process traditionally called *strategic planning*. However, this is only one approach to strategy formation. You may also develop competitive strategies in response to rather than in anticipation of environmental conditions or by taking small steps, revising your approach, learning from your mistakes, and revising again in an iterative process. Or you may be a visionary, entrepreneurial leader who more often than not has guessed right in the past, so when you point your organization in a new direction, your board and staff are likely to give you the benefit of the doubt and follow. These are all common, legitimate ways of forming strategy, and they are not mutually exclusive.

If competition is the process by which different entities vie for limited resources, competitive strategy is, essentially, how they go about accumulating and using advantages while minimizing disadvantages relative to other entities (the process of gaining and using a competitive advantage). In most nonprofit enterprises, competition, either implicitly or explicitly, is a key driver in the formation of organizational strategy ("we must respond to a competitive threat posed by a new nonprofit in the community") and an important tool for carrying out that strategy ("we will win that corporate sponsor"). Competition is not, however, central to most programmatic strategies.

Organizational and Programmatic Strategies

You seek the customers, funders, talented employees, media attention, political clout, and other resources that your competitors also seek. Competition is thus, inevitably, the process of seeking strategic advantage *over other organizations*. When you mount a campaign to recruit a big name in the community as your next new board member, you are, consciously or unconsciously, looking for a strategic advantage over all other nonprofits on whose boards of directors, if you are successful, that person will not serve.

This argument holds true only in regard to organizationally focused strategies, the subject of this book. Specifically programmatic strategies, however, such as those that focus on eradicating poverty or improving educational performance, are bigger than any particular organization. They are essentially the expression of social movements, and therefore do not inherently involve competition between organizations.

For example, you may decide that your nonprofit's strategy for promoting math literacy entails offering after-school tutorials. That is a programmatic strategy. You may also decide that a part of your competitive strategy to attract resources is to position your nonprofit as a recognized community leader and that in order to do that you must attract high-profile board members. That is an organizational strategy. What distinguishes organizational strategies is that they are directed toward gaining resources, while programmatic strategies are directly aimed at addressing the social issues that are the focus of the organization's mission.

Within the realm of programmatic strategies, it is possible that different social movements—for example, the effort to eradicate cancer and that to find a cure for juvenile diabetes—may become competitors for limited resources, such as federal research funds. Even within one movement, different camps or submovements may compete. Consider the long-running argument within the HIV/AIDS-fighting community over whether to raise reserve funds to sustain organizations for a long battle or to expend all funds immediately to serve as many people in crisis as possible. When different movements or different factions of a movement vie for resources, these movements are acting like organizations; they are competing for advantage.

With regard to organizational strategies, what is strategy about but gaining advantage in the quest for resources? If resources—money for example—were unlimited, what need would you have for organizational strategy? When you needed money, you would simply go to the bank and make a withdrawal. It is the limited supply of a resource that creates competition for it, and it is the need to compete successfully for limited resources that leads to the formation of competitive strategies.

However your organizational strategies are arrived at, they are inherently competitive. You decide to move into a new geographic area, hoping to win both customers and funders away from other nonprofits already working there. You build an operating reserve so that you will have the flexibility and stability both to withstand economic downturns and, in good times, to expand programs. You shift directions or begin a new program, hoping to win funds while still pursuing your mission.

Why Compete?

Since you develop and pursue strategies in order to attract resources, the more competitive your environment (the more highly contested the limited pool of resources) is, the more important it is for you to develop strategies that will bring you competitive advantages over other entities. I can imagine that this statement may not sit well with some readers. You may be thinking, "Yes, I know we must compete for limited resources, but that doesn't necessarily imply that we want to gain an advantage over other nonprofits. I may work for one nonprofit, but I support the work of many others in our community, and I do not want to hurt them! Is this inevitable?"

This is a fair question; here is my response. A piecemeal approach to competition (competing for a specific grant or board member) will inevitably pit your nonprofit against others in what appears to be limited ways. That is, you compete over *this* grant or *that* potential board member. So long as your view of competition remains piecemeal, you need not see yourself as broadly competing for advantage against other nonprofits. But that is still what you are doing, because a nonprofit does not compete for each grant or board member in isolation. There is, in fact, a bigger picture, and a great deal is at stake. An example will help to illustrate the point.

Let's suppose that over a one-year period, five nonprofits working in the same field in a community all apply in response to five different requests for proposals. Your nonprofit is one of them. In responding to these RFPs, do you hope to receive only your "fair share" of the available awards—perhaps only one of them—so that the available resources are distributed evenly? Not likely. Instead, you hope to win as many of these competitive processes as possible. Why? Do you consciously wish to harm the other nonprofits? Again, this is unlikely. They are all part of your community and are working on goals that are closely related to yours. In fact, each of the nonprofits is likely to wish the others well in general. However, you still hope to win all the different competitions. Why? Because you recognize that there is more at stake in winning the awards than simply putting money in the bank. If you win a disproportionate share of these competitions, you are likely to view this success as a general endorsement by local funders of your programs, leadership, and reputation, and with good reason.

By standing out from the similar-service pack, the successful competitor not only gains immediate resources, but in the longer term, it positions itself to attract a variety of additional resources. As it differentiates itself, it is likely to grow more quickly than others. Growth may contribute to a more influential role in defining how the field develops, which services will be offered, and which will fall from favor. The successful competitor is more likely to work closely with third-party payers, who will view it as a leader in its field. Such an organization will also find it easier to attract the "A list" board members whom all the nonprofits in town want. The organization's success may secure positive media coverage, which further reinforces its differentiated position, spreading its message and its fundraising reach to a wider audience. Over time, the organization's success may even begin to lure talented staff away from other nonprofits. Each of these benefits is a multiplier of the direct benefits of winning several of the funding competitions. This is why the nonprofit leaders in our example will compete avidly: because much more than a specific grant is at stake.

If we leave aside for a moment the question of intent, you can see that the actual impact of winning most or all of the competitions is that the four unsuccessful competitors are disadvantaged in direct proportion to the advantages accruing to the winner through its success. You may not consciously set out to obtain advantage over your colleagues, and most nonprofit leaders are loath to speak of such intentions openly even if they do harbor them. Yet the unavoidable consequence of competition is that someone gains an advantage while someone else loses it.

Although on one level competition is a process of vying for tangible resources, it is also, on another level, a process of differentiation, branding, and positioning in the minds of potential third-party payers, political allies, and customers. In other words, you may compete for a particular grant in the near term, but you will also eventually compete for name recognition, media coverage, and the development of a brand name and positive reputation familiar to both your current and potential constituents and supporters. Competition is a vehicle not just for directly and immediately procuring resources but also for strengthening your organization's overall position in the intermediate to long term. It is critical to compete successfully because, as much as we might like there to be enough precious resources to go around, the resource pie is simply not going to feed all the nonprofits at the table.

Limited Resources or a Growing Pie?

Nonprofits and their funders like to talk about "growing the pie"—that is, enlarging the overall pool of dollars (board members, qualified staff, or other resources) so that everyone can get a share. This sentiment helps everyone to avoid acknowledging the unpleasant reality that decision makers must choose among many worthy nonprofits. It represents a sincere desire of many in the sector to be inclusive, but from a practical perspective, growing the pie as an antidote to competition is frankly unrealistic.

While it is true that the resources available to your specific issue in your community may grow over time, they are unlikely to do so at a scale or pace that is going to lessen competition as a concern for your nonprofit. In other words, growth in the supply of available resources is never going to match growth in the need or demand for them. Remember that the resources in question are not just monetary. First-rate board members, volunteers and staff, and positive media attention are also limited resources. Continually and rapidly growing the pie of each of these resources would be necessary to keep up with the needs of an ever-growing number of nonprofits. In most times, the resource pie will indeed grow, but it simply will not do so in a way that will lessen the need for competition.

More Than My Share

The slices of the pie, whatever the size, will not be distributed evenly, much as some of us might wish it. This is, after all, America, where a strange concoction of hard work; class status; racial, ethnic, and gender prejudice; social connections; and plain old luck determine relative shares of any pie, whatever the size. Any parent understands the aversion to competitive dynamics experienced by much of the nonprofit sector. When one child asks us to attend a school event at the same time that another child has a soccer game, we have competition. How can we decide between these two activities? As parents, we go through great mental (and sometimes physical) contortions to avoid choosing one event and thus one child over another. We enlist another parent or relative for the soccer game, trade off something else later on, or split our time, attending part of the school event and then making a mad dash across town to see the second half of the soccer game. In these ways, we try to make the situation noncompetitive for our children. In the nonprofit world, we often feel like a parent caught between two children. We care about many causes and want them all to thrive. In the final analysis, we feel we are all on the same side.

Competition needs no justification in the business world. Indeed, the need to compete rarely warrants a second thought; the profit motive sees to that. The businessperson realizes that a contract that she wins is one the competition will not get. The reigning sentiment seems to be that if our win weakens a competitor overall, even to the point of threatening its viability, it is only a bigger plus for us, unless, of course, it signals the demise of an industry or market. After all, fewer competitors means more market share for the survivors and a lower threat to their own viability going forward. If there is an unmet need as a result of the failure of a competitor, the remaining businesses are more than happy to step in to fill it themselves. That is how business leaders—but not most nonprofit leaders—are trained to think.

A Healthy Ecology

You may find that your attitudes are somewhere between those of the harried parent in the earlier example and the businessperson just described. Your organization needs to attract resources, and this usually means attracting them at the expense of other nonprofits. At the same time, you recognize and value the work of your competitors, who most often are also your colleagues, and you do not usually want to see them weakened or leaving the business. This last sentiment also reflects your enlightened self-interest. For example, three health centers in a given community may compete for a new federal contract, which contract may be essential to the ongoing viability of each of the centers. If, after one center is awarded the contract, the other two find it necessary to close their doors, the impact on the community and in particular on the workload of the successful competitor, which must now absorb their patients, would be devastating. Thus, nonprofits compete for resources, but usually not "to the death."

In the nonprofit world, competitors are also an integral part of a social ecology that is healthiest when there are a variety of strong and vibrant players—not a plethora of small, weak operators but enough variety to offer customers a choice, to encourage ongoing innovation, and to cover the diversity of expressed needs. Few thoughtful and mission-focused nonprofit leaders would desire a Microsoft-like monopolistic hegemony in their field. The tension between competitive forces (the need to acquire resources from a limited supply) and ecological forces (the need for several organizations addressing a range of interrelated needs) puts nonprofits in a unique and difficult competitive spot. What is a nonprofit leader to do?

Ethical Competition

Increasingly, nonprofit leaders embrace the need to pursue competitive advantages over others in their field as the best way to gain the resources that their missions require. However, the ecological concerns just discussed require them to adhere to a thoughtful and uniquely nonprofit ethical approach to competition. To accept the need to gain a competitive advantage over others, a nonprofit leader must hold three beliefs:

1. Our cause is righteous.
2. Our organization is capable and effective.
3. We can accomplish additional good results, given the necessary resources.

If your social cause is valuable (and you wouldn't work at your nonprofit if it were not); if you have sound strategies, good leadership, and a track record of success; and if you have a compelling vision of the good you can accomplish with additional resources, then you not only can but *should* choose to compete aggressively to attract the resources you need. Remember the competitive imperative that I presented in the introduction to Part One: a nonprofit with a righteous cause, a sound organization, and a compelling vision faces an ethical imperative to do more: to help more people, preserve more of nature, produce more beauty, protect more people's rights, and so on. Failing to do so is tantamount to accepting that your nonprofit will not maximize the social benefit it was created to provide. The following four precepts may be helpful in understanding this competitive imperative.

1. *Constructive competition is good for everyone.* You can best help sustain a healthy ecology within your community by competing ethically *and* aggressively for the resources you need. If you offer a high-quality program that meets a real need, competition leads you to showcase your successes, attracting resources such as board members, staff, or foundation grants, which prefer to associate themselves with successful enterprises. Such competition raises the bar for the entire field.

2. *We are only as strong as our weakest link.* No cause is advanced when a nonprofit with little ability to perform uses up resources. This nonprofit is taking resources from those that could make better use of it. We all know of instances where for political, philosophical, or historical reasons, nonprofits continue to secure funds, to attract board members, and even to receive positive media attention, despite a near total inability to perform. Most often these nonprofits will eventually fail, sometimes spectacularly, but not until they have wasted precious resources, sometimes over many years, and often brought ignominy to their community or the entire sector.

3. *Darwin works here.* If yours is an effective nonprofit, you have an ethical obligation to try to attract the resources you need to advance your mission, even by wresting resources away from poor performers. While the resource pool available to your issue and community is not a perfect zero-sum game, neither is it endlessly elastic, as we have seen. Funding is severely limited. Media interest in most nonprofit issues is transitory at best, and many worthy causes vie for the best staff and board members. In this environment, there must be a winnowing out of weak performers so that the strong can thrive.

4. *Power to the people who can deliver.* The nonprofit world is indeed a competitive marketplace. You compete in a market where the usual business forces are not suspended; in fact, they apply in spades. Common economic pressures—to

produce, to grow, to innovate, and respond to customers—are all alive and well in the nonprofit sector. They are complicated, however, by a general paucity of resources and additional value-derived political and social forces that can be pronounced. The combination of normal economic pressures and these social and political forces makes nonprofit leadership especially difficult. Nonetheless, it is in this complicated world that you must compete on multiple levels. You ignore this fact at the peril of your organization's mission.

The Consequences of Competition

Obviously, there are both positive and negative potential consequences associated with the particular competitive environment that your nonprofit faces, and, in particular, with adopting an organizational strategy of greater competitiveness. Some of the consequences of competitiveness that you might experience are similar to those associated with competitiveness in the business world. In each sector, the particular nature of the competitive environment in which various organizations must vie for limited resources brings both special opportunities and concerns. Let's look first at similarities between the challenges of competition in nonprofits and in business; then we will look at some unique challenges facing nonprofits.

Shared Business-Nonprofit Competitive Challenges

Competition can bring a focus and strength to your efforts, but in each sector there are also potential downsides if competitive forces are not balanced by striving for something bigger. In the business world, that might be a legacy, a technological revolution, or a founder's personal goal. In the nonprofit world, the task of identifying the "something bigger" is much easier, even automatic; it is your organization's mission.

Acknowledging that the nonprofit sector, too, is a competitive world is only the first step. Table 2.1 displays five broad competitive challenges shared by businesses and nonprofits. For each challenge, the table describes both a pro, or potential positive consequence to the organization of facing this challenge, and a con, or potential negative consequence the organization may experience by trying to address the particular competitive challenge. Generally, the con is most likely to be experienced by an organization if competitive forces are not tempered by strong leadership and balanced by principled, mission-driven management, starting at the very top, with the chief executive and the board.

TABLE 2.1. COMPETITIVE CHALLENGES SHARED BY BUSINESSES AND NONPROFITS.

Challenge	Pro (Advantage of Competition)	Con, or Risk (Disadvantage of Competition)
Productivity	The drive toward greater work efficiency leads to growth and economic strength in the long term.	Inhumane and thus counterproductive treatment of employees can result in lower quality and higher cost in the long term.
Innovation	The need for ongoing innovation keeps people engaged and produces greater value for customers.	Management pushing too hard and too quickly can lead to a temptation to fudge results in order to achieve unrealistic deadlines and goals.
Quality	Better-quality products and services are produced, and increased value is brought to the consumer.	Striving for perfection can lead to not getting on with the work, losing sight of economic realities, or sacrificing the morale of employees.
Customer service	Better customer service and increased responsiveness to consumer needs result in customer loyalty.	Competition for customers can lead to a focus on touting service rather than providing it; marketing can outstrip performance.
Cost or value	Competition can result in lower costs to producers or providers and lower prices for consumers or payers without decreasing service or quality.	Skimping on necessary investment to keep costs or prices down can reduce value and ultimately hurt quality and customer service.

The Productivity Challenge

In order to compete successfully over the long haul, both businesses and nonprofits must be productive, making optimum use of limited human and other resources. The need to increase productivity is generally a positive force in both sectors; it leads to greater efficiency, ongoing investment in technological improvements, and ultimately to greater overall economic health for the enterprise and society. It is no coincidence that one of the U.S. economy's most closely watched benchmarks of health is growth or decline in labor productivity.

On the other hand, taken to an extreme, increasing workloads combined with callous disregard for employees—for example, viewing workers as interchangeable parts rather than as partners in the endeavor—can lead to falling morale, lower productivity, and economic crisis for the enterprise and the community. This is as true for your nonprofit as it is for Wal-Mart. While businesses focus far more explicitly on productivity promotion strategies than do nonprofits, the best nonprofits still tend to feel their way along, often intuitively, toward productivity gains. Nonetheless, these potential positive and negative outcomes are common to both sectors.

The Innovation Challenge

Both businesses and nonprofits need to constantly innovate in order to compete effectively in a changing marketplace. Management teams and, in larger business corporations and nonprofits, research and development units (think of pharmaceutical companies, big research universities, and the national offices of groups like the YMCA), are constantly struggling with the right mix of products and services and trying to anticipate the next level of improvement or innovation their customers want before their competitors can bring it out or, as in so many technological breakthroughs, before their customers even realize they need it. (Who would have predicted in 2000 that today some of us would not be able to live without a telephone that is also a digital camera and is small enough to fit in a shirt pocket?) The challenge to innovate is a strong motivator to higher achievement.

On the dark side, creativity cannot always be made to produce concrete results, especially within a specific timetable. Sometimes the need for successful innovation to happen quickly can lead to unethical conduct, such as faking research results or claiming exaggerated benefits for an unproven product or service. A singular focus on innovation can also lead an organization to ignore the needs of its current high-performing lines of business, which may require ongoing investment and attention. Neglecting the known in favor of the unproven "next big thing" has its risks in both sectors. Strong, practical, and moral leadership is essential to avoid this pitfall, which is akin to killing, through neglect, the goose that lays the golden egg. Balance between innovation and ongoing execution is essential in both sectors.

The Quality Challenge

In order to effectively compete, both businesses and nonprofits must consistently deliver an acceptable level of quality in their products or services. Quality is only as high as it is perceived to be by your customers and third-party payers. Quality improvement strategies are common in both sectors. In fact, the quality improvement movement has become something of a religion in American business and to a lesser extent among nonprofits, although the apex of its influence has probably passed. Quality circles, TQM, and the Japanese concept of *kaizen* (continual, incremental improvement), have all made inroads in the nonprofit world. Despite the arms race in the use of superlatives to describe quality, I have consciously chosen to refer to an *acceptable* level of quality as the requirement, rather than *exceptional, outstanding, superior,* or some other form of hyperbole. The challenge is for you to consistently produce a product, activity, or service that meets or exceeds your customer's expectations, and that, we all know, is hard enough.

On the potential negative side of the ledger is the tendency of R&D staff to want to continue improving a new product forever. In this situation, "the perfect is the enemy of the good." Quality concerns must be gauged within an economic reality. "How good is good enough?" is as much an economic question as one of quality. If a product, activity, or service becomes too expensive to deliver, it will not be delivered, no matter how good it might be. Finally, an obsession with quality can burn out staff members who are continually told or have been trained to tell themselves that "it is not yet good enough."

The Customer Service Challenge

One of the smartest moves any business or nonprofit can make in order to increase its competitive edge is to improve its customer service. People complain constantly about poor service in their daily interactions with government, business, and nonprofits alike. The rude postal clerk, the long bank line, the filthy service station restroom, the pushy fundraiser, and the interminable automated phone system at the blood bank are all examples of poor customer service that either drive customers away or at least make people want to minimize their interactions with the offending institution. The challenge, again, is to provide your customers with the level of responsiveness they want and perhaps a little bit more. In the case of nonprofits, responsiveness to third-party payers is, of course, equally important.

Truly high-level customer service is a distinct competitive advantage. On the other hand, both businesses and nonprofits are occasionally prone to spend more time and effort selling potential customers on the quality of their customer service than actually providing a satisfying experience to current customers. This tends to happen in businesses or nonprofits that are operating in highly competitive markets. Marketing may get ahead of performance in this situation. For example, consider the United Way of the Bay Area creation called PipeVine, which boasted a new level of efficiency and donor responsiveness but which, as it closed its doors in mid-2003, announced that it had spent restricted funds intended for nonprofits to cover its own operating costs.

The Cost/Value Challenge

Finally, cost, and the value gained for that cost, is a key competitive dimension in both sectors. If a business or nonprofit is able to deliver to its customers a desired product, activity, or service at an acceptable level of quality for a lower price than the competition and if it markets and communicates these advantages effectively, it will likely win increased market share over time. Thus, an important feature of competition is that it forces prices down. Any enterprise sustainably lowers prices either by lowering its own production unit costs or by increasing sales volume so that it can afford to make a smaller margin on more units sold. Ideally, it will use both approaches.

On the other hand, rampant price reductions in order to reap the rewards of being the low price leader or cost cutting as an act of desperation in response to a new competitor with a lower cost structure or a better product or service can lead you to a failure to invest in people, facilities, equipment, and future ideas (R&D), which will harm your nonprofit in the long run. Such precipitous acts can also lead to a much quicker and more painful end if your organization has inadequate cash reserves. Cash cows can only be milked for so long before they go dry. In extreme cases, price wars can undermine a business's or nonprofit's economic stability and threaten its survival. A theater lowering its ticket prices to attract audience can fill seats in the short run but may bankrupt the organization in the final act.

Competitive Challenges Unique to Nonprofits

In addition to challenges shared by businesses and nonprofits, competition also presents a few challenges that occur only in the nonprofit sector (see Table 2.2). Again, the column designated "Pro" contains some potential positive outcomes of the challenge, while the column labeled "Con" holds the potential negatives.

The Community Involvement Challenge

If your nonprofit competes successfully for the full array of resources it needs and is generally considered by its community, customers, third-party payers, and other constituents to be an excellent actor in its field, it will attract people who are interested in helping to advance its cause in a variety of ways. Potential board members, volunteers, and staff who feel their skills and passion will be put to good use will be inclined to contribute their efforts to a successful nonprofit, advancing their active participation in the community while benefiting your nonprofit and its mission. This is a win-win-win situation for the person in question, for your nonprofit, and for the larger community.

On the other hand, if a nonprofit is perceived by the community as virtually indistinguishable from a business (for example, a theater that is known solely for its direct-from-Broadway productions and that offers no educational or charitable programs in the community), it will not tend to attract volunteers or donors.

TABLE 2.2. COMPETITIVE CHALLENGES UNIQUE TO NONPROFITS.

Challenge	Pro (Advantage of competition)	Con (Disadvantage of Competition)
Community involvement	Succeeding through competition can raise an organization's profile and attract people to its activities (board, volunteers, and staff choose to work for a winner), promoting their civic participation.	If the nonprofit is not distinguishable from a business enterprise, there can be a loss of community involvement (board members go elsewhere) or staff commitment (the best staff leave). The uniqueness of a nonprofit must be preserved.
Mission	The skills necessary to successfully compete will sharpen a nonprofit's focus, giving it an edge in mission advancement.	If competition focuses on the bottom line rather than mission advancement (an easy trap to fall into), it can crowd out mission focus, doing irreparable harm to the nonprofit in the long run.
Public perception	Nonprofits that use a competitive strategy have the opportunity to be seen as businesslike and responsible.	Overtly competitive nonprofits run the risk of being seen as cutthroat, noncollaborative, or elitist.

The unique "nonprofitness" of a nonprofit, to use Paul Light's term (Light, 2002b), must shine through in order for the general community to be attracted to your enterprise as volunteers, supporters, donors, and employees.

The Mission Challenge

Aggressive competition can bring a new level of resources to your nonprofit, allowing it to pursue its social mission with increased vigor. This is important because it is no secret that many nonprofits lack the critical mass of capital and other resources necessary to have much of an impact on their identified social issue. Often, these nonprofits fail to advance their missions very far over time not because of poor ideas, weak programs, or unmotivated people but simply due to a lack of resources to develop and implement their ideas at a scale capable of achieving a significant impact.

If successful competition helps a small but otherwise successful nonprofit to grow, mission advancement often results. Competition can be good for the mission! Clara Miller (2003), in that rare article on nonprofit finance that is actually fun to read, argues that there are three elements of nonprofit success: mission; organizational capacity; and having an appropriate capital structure, including cash, physical assets, and investments. Success requires much more than having a good idea and motivated people; it also requires an appropriate level of resources.

Alternatively, we have discussed the perils of mission creep—seeking resources at the expense of remaining focused on mission. Similarly, an exclusive focus on the bottom line can lead, for a time, to a financially successful but morally bankrupt nonprofit. To avoid this pitfall, competition must always be toward a social end, not a financial end in itself.

The Public Perception Challenge

The public is a bit schizophrenic in its view of nonprofits. On one hand, we hear the constant cries of corporate supporters and the public at large that nonprofits should become more businesslike, which implies having adequate resources to manage and perform well (Miller's capital structure). On the other hand, we hear a steady stream of criticism of nonprofits becoming too corporate: paying their executives too lavishly, spending too much on offices, losing their nonprofit look and feel, and their essentially charitable (donative) nature. Thus, by becoming an aggressive competitor, your nonprofit can gain public recognition for pursuing a successful, competitive business model, only to fall victim to the criticism that it is building an empire, elitist, commercial, and unwilling to collaborate with other nonprofits. Indeed, a delicate balance and a fine sense for the appearance as well as the substance of various actions and policies is necessary to navigate through these challenges. Competition is, after all, in addition to all else we have described, an ethical, cultural and political act.

The adoption of an organizational strategy of increased competitiveness has ethical and cultural implications for a nonprofit, in addition to the more obvious strategic and economic ones, making it a supremely important and highly political business decision. Let's take a brief look at the ethical and cultural ramifications you will face.

The Politics of Competition

In the nonprofit world, political concerns are usually thought to involve policy struggles, as in the passage or defeat of a piece of legislation, but here I am referring to something altogether different. As the leader of a nonprofit considering an increasingly competitive stance in the world, you face ethical and cultural challenges on a regular basis. These challenges are small "p" political because they can cause disunity among your board, staff, and other key constituents. Let's look first at the ethical issues that arise and then at the cultural issues.

Ethical Implications

As I have stated, it is only ethical to seek a share of a limited resource if you can make effective use of it in addressing an identified challenge or advancing a worthwhile cause. The problem for most nonprofit leaders lies not in accepting this premise but rather in operationalizing it by seeing their organization accurately and being fully aware of their own motivations. Nonprofit leaders, being human, have a tendency to see their organization and in particular their own actions in a more positive light than might perhaps be warranted. Closely related to nonprofit leaders' rosy perspective is their strong instinct for self-preservation, for keeping their organization going and their loyal, hardworking staff employed. This instinct can develop into a perceived mandate to feed the organization resources whether it is doing an effective job or not. (Recall the earlier discussion of mission creep.)

You probably know from experience the results of wearing blinders about your own weaknesses, either personally, as a manager, or as an entire organization. I have also discussed the problems inherent in acting primarily in order to preserve your organization. In either case, the result is wasted resources and operational problems that continue to pile up unaddressed. You can use board members and colleagues as a sounding board, but you must also rely on your own sense of right and wrong to counter the natural human tendency to continue doing what you have been doing, despite indications that it is not working. Failure to pay attention to these challenges can lead to the development of factions on your board or among your staff: those who want (sometimes dramatic) change and those who cling to the status quo.

The process recommended in Chapter Four can help you to take a dispassionate look at your organization's position. If it is simply too difficult for your board and staff to undertake this examination for themselves (which is a legitimate conclusion to draw), you may want to engage a consultant to conduct an organizational assessment, using one of many widely available tools.

In any event, it is imperative that you adopt a first priority of achieving all that is possible with the resources available to you, before seeking more. In the resource-starved nonprofit world, there is a great temptation to label every problem as being due to a shortage of some essential commodity. While this view contains more than a grain of truth—in fact, having more resources is often helpful with many challenges—it is not wise to begin there. Operational or governance problems generally are not fixed by enlarging the budget and may even be exacerbated by the greater complications that more money or a larger staff brings to an organization. When a nonprofit leader complains of having inadequate funds, it may be because his organization has neither the track record nor the vision to attract resources. To compete ethically and successfully, the first principle must be to act responsibly and effectively with available resources, attempting to grow as a unifying process of building on strengths, not as a way to escape from weaknesses.

Cultural Implications

Adopting an organizational strategy of increased competitiveness represents, for many nonprofits, a major change from the status quo. As we saw in Chapter One, even beginning to think competitively, let alone act competitively, can be countercultural in many nonprofits. Thus, one of the major consequences of starting down an overtly competitive path will be the change process that your nonprofit will need to experience. You are likely to encounter resistance from staff members and perhaps also from board members. You may also be subject to accusations of selling out and impassioned assertions that "we are not a business" from staff, volunteers, customers, and other constituents who are somewhat distant from the economic challenges that you face.

People who take this view may think of the organization exclusively in terms of its mission, seeing only its programmatic face and refusing to acknowledge that the mission advancement challenge also has an economic and therefore a competitive face. Constituents often view their nonprofit not as an organization but as an entity coextensive with the delivery of the current mix of programs. They may resist, on principle, examining some of the questions raised in this book.

While a great deal of energy may go into formulating an understanding of your organization's place in the market and from there to developing competitive strategies—essentially Parts Two and Three of this book—you must also build in time and energy to work through this change process, or your efforts are likely to stall. Change expert William Bridges writes, in the opening of his classic treatment of organizational transitions: "It isn't the changes that do you in, it's the transitions" (1991, p. 3). The difficult part of any change is the *movement* from a cherished if dysfunctional old position to an unknown new one. In this case, the shift from a relatively low level of competitiveness to a higher one can be a wrenching change, so getting there may entail a painful transition.

One long-term approach that can help a great deal with this dynamic is to bring all of your staff and as many other constituents as possible to a higher level of understanding of your organization's economic situation. Ask your program managers to develop and submit budgets rather than developing them centrally yourself. Then ask them to participate in monitoring their own expenses by reviewing monthly accounting reports. Offer training, support, and guidance as they do this. Ask them in turn to work with their frontline staff as they develop and monitor their budgets. They will quickly learn how little money there is, where it comes from, and how few line items their senior leadership has any real control over. (For example, salaries, rent, and utilities are fixed and often represent 80 percent or more of the organization's budget.) Engage your board and staff in other economically focused discussions as well. For example, try an exercise of describing the other organizations in your field; develop an understanding of what each does, how it is funded, and how the ecology of the field fits together. Over time, this approach can build a better understanding across the organization of competitive forces in the market, of your nonprofit's budget, and of its underlying business model. Knowledge of this sort makes it easier to see the need for change, even if the transition, as Bridges asserts, will still be quite difficult.

Conclusion

Competition is a critical dynamic in your nonprofit's strategic life. It brings the possibility of helping your organization to stand out from the crowd, and it can lead to better organizational efforts and better outcomes for customers. But just as collaboration is not a one-size-fits-all solution to your problems, neither is competition a panacea. A range of options on both sides of the spectrum of collaborative and competitive relationships is necessary for success. Let's move on to consider a new way of looking at both collaboration and competition among nonprofits: as parts of a complex spectrum of relationships.

CHAPTER THREE

THE COMPETITIVE CONTINUUM

This chapter provides a view of competition and collaboration as interrelated aspects of nonprofit competitive strategy. The goal here is to demonstrate the different forms of relatedness that occur between and among nonprofits and to provide tools for measuring that relatedness and determining what it means for strategy. It can be difficult and confusing to determine a nonprofit's optimal relationship with others in its market. You may struggle at times to understand the different competitive and collaborative relationships that must coexist in your world. This chapter provides a framework for making these determinations.

The Range of Nonprofit Relationships: Working Together

We saw in Chapter One that nonprofits relate to one another across a spectrum of collaborative relationships. I have previously modeled these relationships from the informally collaborative to the increasingly integrative, culminating in merger (La Piana, 2000). A greatly simplified version of La Piana Associates' Nonprofit Partnership Matrix, which details the range of collaborative relationships, is shown in Table 3.1.

Collaboration tends to be informal and episodic. When, for example, a budget cut from a common funder threatens a group of nonprofits, they join together to fight it. When the crisis passes, however, the perceived need to work together also

TABLE 3.1. SIMPLIFIED NONPROFIT PARTNERSHIP MATRIX.

Collaboration	Strategic Alliance	Corporate Integration
• Informal • Relatively low level • Episodic • Often program-focused	• Formal • More involved • Driven by a written agreement • Intended to be long-lasting	• Formal • Involves legal changes to partners' structure • Intended to be permanent

subsides. Strategic alliances, in contrast, are more formal, driven by a written agreement, and are intended to endure. An example would be an agreement for one nonprofit to provide others with accounting services. Alliances require a great deal of work both to develop and to maintain. Corporate integration, the most intense form of partnership, involves changes to the corporate structure of the participants or the creation of a new, related entity. For example, three nonprofits may create a management services organization, separately incorporated and jointly controlled, to perform their administrative functions, or two nonprofits may decide to merge.

While the Nonprofit Partnership Matrix as shown in Table 3.1 provides a framework for thinking about collaborative relationships among nonprofits, it tells only half of the strategic story. Rather than create a parallel matrix modeling competitive relationships, I found that both collaborative and competitive relationships can be modeled along the same dimensions and that the resulting matrix yields a more holistic and complex understanding of nonprofit strategy.

The Nonprofit Strategy Matrix

The three-level, increasingly intense model of collaborative nonprofit relationships provides a useful framework for describing the levels of competitive relationships your nonprofit may experience. In fact, nonprofit collaboration and competition can be plotted along the same spectrum as options at any point in the progression from less intense to more intense relationships. This formulation is depicted in the Nonprofit Strategy Matrix (Figure 3.1).

The need for competition, like the need for collaboration, is constantly changing; competitive threats and opportunities as well as other market conditions continually evolve, and periodically undergo moments of transformation. The Nonprofit Strategy Matrix can help you to understand the range of possible relationships among nonprofits. This understanding can help you to make the right choices, given the conditions that may apply at any given moment. As you

FIGURE 3.1. NONPROFIT STRATEGY MATRIX.

Competitive Purpose		
• Grantseeking • Board recruitment • Staff recruitment • Volunteer recruitment • Sponsorships	• Controlling market share • Freezing out competitors • Entering new market • Defining market niche • Creating a service continuum	• Gaining market share • Acquiring another organization • Eliminating a competitor • Driving an organization from market • Driving an organization from business

Level of Intensity of Relationship		
Low Intensity Using incidental or occasional strategies to achieve desired ends	**Medium Intensity** Using strategic alliances to achieve desired ends	**High Intensity** Using integrative or exclusive strategies to achieve desired ends

Collaborative Purpose		
• Collaborative fundraising • Shared political activity • Cooperative service provision • Information sharing • Group purchasing	• Consolidating administration • Joint programming • Sharing services • Exchanging services • Reducing cost	• Merging missions • Merging administrative services • Sharing ownership of an asset • Leveraging another organization's assets • Unifying control of a market or resource

review the matrix, remember that none of these choices is permanent and most are not even mutually exclusive.

Your nonprofit, of course, relates to businesses and government units as well as to other nonprofits; these relationships can also be understood using the Nonprofit Strategy Matrix. By "intensity of relationship," I mean the frequency, depth, and overall strategic importance of the interactions or competitive conflicts between and among organizations. Like most nonprofits, yours probably routinely has fairly low-intensity relationships with a wide variety of organizations: businesses, nonprofits, and government. You also probably have more intense relationships with a small number of groups, creating strategic alliances that are important to your (and their) overall mission advancement. Finally, you may occasionally enter into very intense relationships that affect your organization's independence and even its continued existence as a separate entity—for example, a merger with another nonprofit.

At the low intensity level, nonprofits use what I call incidental or occasional strategies to achieve ends that may be either competitive or collaborative. Incidental strategies are specific, often episodic, and largely unintended; thus, they are incidental rather than purposeful. Seeking foundation grants constitutes an incidental competitive strategy for gaining resources. It is not a strategy vis-à-vis other nonprofits; it is simply, as we have seen, an inherently competitive thing to do, because the funder has limited grantmaking dollars. This mundane activity hardly merits the term *strategy*, but it does meet the definition I have been using: a pattern of behavior that constitutes a way of moving an organization toward its goals. Other incidental competitive strategies include efforts at board member or staff recruitment. Because these are limited resources, it is inherently but not deliberately competitive to recruit people for any role with your nonprofit. Collaborative strategies, on the other hand, do not occur incidentally. Working together requires intentionality. It doesn't just happen on its own.

Occasional competitive strategies arise, for example, when you vie with other nonprofits over an RFP issued by a common funder. There may be intense competition for the award, but once the winner is decided, the relationships among the contenders usually return to the previous state. I call these strategies "occasional" because they are specific to the occasion and do not usually result in lasting changes in your relationships with other entities. Nonetheless, as we saw earlier, winning these competitions can have a profound cumulative effect on your stature in the community and your future ability to attract a wide range of contested resources.

Occasional collaborative strategies abound. A joint response to an RFP or the annual county-level budget battle both qualify. Executive roundtables, group purchasing plans, and informal coordinated service provision are all examples of occasional, specific collaboration for a defined purpose. Another way to describe occasional collaboration or competition is that it has no "legs"; it is limited in both scope and time.

At the medium intensity level, nonprofits form alliances to achieve desired ends that are usually quite clearly specified. The hallmark of a strategic alliance is that it is fairly formal, usually guided by a written agreement (either a contract or a memorandum of understanding signed by the parties), and it is intended to be long-lasting. Alliances arise for a variety of purposes. An alliance is primarily competitive in nature when it is intended to seek an external, market advantage. For example, you might join with a group of nonprofits to form an alliance intended to exert greater influence in the market and by so doing to improve your competitive position, particularly in regard to pricing. Your group may also form an alliance in order to scare off potential new market entrants. A potential competitor who sees what is essentially a cartel situation, in which an established group of nonprofits has already secured the best government contracts and thus locked up the market, may decide it is simply not worth the fight to try to break into your market and thus look for opportunities elsewhere, where there is less competition, less expense, and less risk.

A group of nonprofits may also form an alliance in order to reduce risk when entering a new market. When a group of California nonprofits providing residential treatment for abused children decided to combine their efforts to provide, through foster homes, a level of care that was then available only at their campus-based programs, they formed an alliance to minimize their risk. As it happens, this alliance was also used to define a new market niche. When the major players in any field get together to try a new approach, the power of their total market share and influence can weigh heavily in the definition of a new niche or position, which they then try to occupy together.

Finally, an alliance can be used to develop a comprehensive scope of services that is hard for anyone outside of the alliance to compete with. Frequently, nonprofits do not need to compete for additional customers because there are far more people in need of what they offer than they can collectively serve. Instead, they compete for the resources to serve their own customers while collaboratively urging decision makers to provide the resources to serve more people. If they succeed, they then compete with one another for those additional resources.

A business analogy might help to clarify this point. Far more people at any given time would like to buy a new car—and really need a new car—than can afford a new car. Automobile manufacturers do not compete for people who want to buy a new car; they compete for people who can afford to buy one and therefore are going to buy one. They may also work together through their industry trade groups to lobby for changes in laws or financing arrangements that would make it easier for more people to buy cars. If they succeed in these joint political efforts, they will then compete for those new customers who enter the market.

On the collaborative side of the Nonprofit Strategy Matrix, strategic alliances are used to build internal strengths (as opposed to the external advantages sought on the competitive side). For example, alliances can be used to consolidate administrative functions such as financial, information technology, and human resources management among nonprofits (Kohm, La Piana, and Gowdy, 2000, p. 11). Alliances are used to enter into collaborative programming arrangements, where staff from the different nonprofits work as one, combining their unique skills in a service that none could provide as easily or economically on its own.

Alliances can help you to share services, as when a group of organizations negotiates with an auditor to serve each of its members at a discounted price. Exchanges of services are less common but do occur. A nonprofit with a human resources director on staff might exchange her services for those of an in-house technology person at another organization. A common purpose of all these collaborative strategic alliances is to save funds or to improve administrative efficiency for the participating members.

It is entirely possible for a strategic alliance to be at once collaborative (focused on building internal strengths) and competitive (focused on gaining external advantages). In fact, these ends may be mutually reinforcing. You may initially join forces with a group of nonprofits in order to freeze out a potential new competitor, then find that in order to do so you must become more efficient by sharing some administrative functions—for example, by establishing a joint box office or billing function. This arrangement may in turn lead you to consider creating a more seamless continuum among your programs, which may eventually force still greater internal coordination. This seesaw developmental cycle may lead to a dense web of purposes, both collaborative among your partners and competitive against outsiders (see Figure 3.2).

Finally, at the high intensity level of relationships, your nonprofit may use integrative or exclusive strategies to achieve its desired ends. Integrative strategies are intended to bring different organizations together, as in a merger. Exclusive strategies are intended, on the competitive side of the matrix, to lock or force a competitor out of a market.

Your nonprofit may try to strengthen its market position by reducing competition. This can be accomplished through actions that pressure a competitor to opt out of the market or even out of business (exclusive strategies). For example, heavy marketing to attract customers or other key resources to your organization can force your competitors to also increase their marketing or risk losing their current share of those resources. For some groups, particularly those with a thin operating margin, this added expense may make what was already a financially marginal activity untenable. The rational response for them may be to leave the market.

Other, more dramatic competitive moves can also up the ante to a point where a competitor decides to drop out of a market—for example, implementing the very

FIGURE 3.2. ALLIANCE DEVELOPMENT.

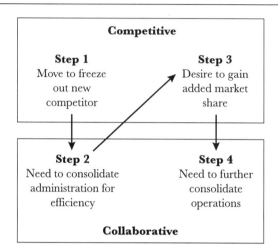

risky decision to lower prices, even below costs, for a time. A cash-rich organization might decide to do this in order to essentially buy market share. A cash-poor organization is unlikely to be able to follow suit and may be forced to abandon the market. Actions such as these are highly risky. Once prices are lowered, it may be difficult to raise them again, and a nonprofit that is seen to be actively driving competitors from its market risks being considered predatory. As in all strategic decision making, before undertaking such high-risk moves, you must ask yourself whether they are ethical and what kind of public impression they will create—two separate questions—as well as whether they are good business decisions.

Competition can also be reduced through a merger or acquisition, in which a competitor is brought into the fold of the acquirer (an integrative strategy) and thus no longer presents a competitive threat. Here is an example, slightly changed to protect the anonymity of the protagonists. Two ballet companies compete each Christmas season, when families turn out in large numbers for sentimental favorites, cash cows that see the companies through the rest of the year. Production of *The Nutcracker* provides one group with a substantial portion of its annual income. The other company tries to wrest away from it the only venue in town large enough to make either group's Christmas production profitable. Since the venue is under city control, this decision is political. Rather than trust to the political process, where it might lose big, the Nutcracker company instead initiates merger discussions with its rival, which is financially weaker. Ultimately, the two companies agree to merge, ending organizational competition for the disputed space. The merged entity can now determine the best use of the space and the revenues it generates.

Nonprofit (and for-profit) competitors can also be persuaded, on occasion, to voluntarily quit a particular market. This can be done, as MacMillan (1983) suggests, by offering a program exchange to the competitor: lower-priority programs are exchanged for ones that each party values more highly. In this way, each nonprofit plays to its strengths and reduces its competition at the same time. If a competitor is not amenable to such an exchange, or if it has nothing you consider worth trading for, then a more aggressive attempt to win resources away may be undertaken (either an exclusive or an integrative strategy may be pursued).

On the collaborative side of the Nonprofit Strategy Matrix, high-intensity relationships are usually integrative. Nonprofits with very similar program activities may merge in order to pursue their similar missions, to fully bring together administrative services for efficiencies, or, quite often, for both reasons. Other nonprofits may merge to unify control over a disparate set of programs that constitute a fragmented market. Yet another group of nonprofits may merge in order to leverage one another's core competencies or assets, as when a K–8 private school merges with a private high school, forming a seamless continuum of curriculum and admissions that is appealing to parents and students alike. Alternatively, rather than a merger, two or more nonprofits may create a jointly controlled subsidiary corporation in order to share ownership of an important asset while reducing each group's individual risk—for example, in order to buy a building.

Figure 3.3 shows the range of strategies available at each level of intensity of relationship on both the competitive and collaborative sides of the Nonprofit Strategy Matrix. Collaborative purposes can be advanced through occasional strategies, strategic alliances, and integrative strategies, each available at their respective level of intensity. These same classes of strategies are available for

FIGURE 3.3. SIMPLIFIED NONPROFIT STRATEGY MATRIX.

Competitive Purpose	• Incidental strategies • Occasional strategies	• Strategic alliances	• Exclusive strategies • Integrative strategies
Level of Intensity of Relationship	**Low Intensity**	**Medium Intensity**	**High Intensity**
Collaborative Purpose	• Occasional strategies	• Strategic alliances	• Integrative strategies

competitive purposes, augmented at the low-intensity end by incidental strategies and at the high-intensity end by exclusive strategies.

With the Nonprofit Strategy Matrix in mind, it is now possible to ask what factors cause nonprofits to choose particular strategies for relating to other organizations. What causes them to choose strategies at various levels of intensity on the matrix for either competitive or collaborative purposes? The degree of what might be termed "relatedness" of two organizations may be the deciding factor.

The Organizational Relatedness Index

Organizational relatedness is a measure of how similar two organizations are on four measures: programs, customers, geography, and stakeholders. Let's take an example. A leadership development program for nonprofit executives was approached about a merger with a very similar program. Both provided leadership development services in the same community, although there were some differences in their target populations. The first leadership program, by far the stronger of the two, was faced with the choice of either merging with the other nonprofit (thereby attempting to save the weaker group from insolvency) or rejecting the merger (opting to compete for resources with the weaker nonprofit and thereby hastening its failure).

Either strategy could remove the stronger nonprofit's primary competitor for the limited resources available in its field. Either strategy could work. What the stronger program could not do was simply ignore the other nonprofit. The presence of two highly related organizations, combined with the limited resources available for their work, meant that they were constantly falling over each other in their resource acquisition efforts. Moreover, the two groups created confusion among their supporters, not a good thing for either of them. Thus, they needed to either join forces (an integrative strategy) or fight a competitive battle for resources (an exclusive strategy).

How the two groups would score on the Organizational Relatedness Index is shown in Table 3.2. Adding the scores in each column results in a total score of 13 out of a possible 16, indicating a nearly perfect match. This score indicates that they will need to consider high-intensity strategies for dealing with one another, either collaboratively or competitively. A high degree of relatedness pits organizations against one another for a variety of resources.

The Organizational Relatedness Index is a simple tool for assessing the relatedness—and thus the potential for intense competition or collaboration—between organizations. Organizations can be assigned scores from 1 to 4 for each of the four measures, providing a rough indication of the degree of their relatedness. Let's review each of these dimensions:

TABLE 3.2. ORGANIZATIONAL RELATEDNESS INDEX.

Names of Competitors: "Leadership Group X and Leadership Group Y"

	Score			
	Low	Medium	High	Extreme
Dimension	1	2	3	4
Similarity of programs			X	
Overlap of customers			X	
Overlap of geography				X
Overlap of third-party payers			X	

Similarity of programs. This dimension refers to mission-related programmatic activities. Nonprofits with virtually indistinguishable activities receive a rating of "extreme," while those with similar but distinguishable activities receive a rating of "high." Organizations with somewhat related but quite distinct activities receive a rating of "medium," while largely dissimilar activities receive a rating of "low." In our example, the two leadership programs receive a rating of "high." Their rating would be "extreme" if they offered identical program models, "medium" if perhaps one offered a month-long program and the other a one-day seminar, and "low" if one offered leadership development and the other some other type of activity.

Overlap of customers. This dimension refers to the degree to which different nonprofits offer activities for the same people. If they are the very same people—for example, battered women staying in a shelter who receive counseling from a clinic focusing on the needs of battered women—then the overlap is extreme. If they are very similar populations, with perhaps many overlapping individuals—for example, those people who attend both the opera and the symphony—the overlap is high. If the overlap is medium, it means the populations have similar characteristics but are still quite distinct, such as the women in the shelter above and other low-income women who might receive transitional employment assistance. Low overlap refers to very different populations—for example, women living in shelters and children using after-school care. The leadership programs in our example served different people, but their participants were quite similar and sought similar programs. They receive a rating of "high" on overlap of customers.

Overlap of geography. This dimension is perhaps the easiest to assess. Nonprofits serving the same area, whether that is a neighborhood or a nation, have an extreme level of overlap. Those serving somewhat overlapping geographic areas—for example, a county and a state in which that county resides—have high overlap. A medium level of overlap would be seen in nonprofits with contiguous but not overlapping service areas—for example, organizations serving adjacent neighbor-hoods. A low level of overlap means that the groups serve different areas entirely, even if the nonprofits are located in the same place. For example, a national non-profit organization serving members throughout the country from an office in New York City has low overlap with a locally focused group occupying the same office building. In our leadership program example, the two entities serve the same com-munity, so their geographic overlap is extreme.

Overlap of third-party payers. This dimension looks at the relatedness of two organizations by assessing the overlap of their funders. If the organizations have the same third-party payers—for example, if they are primarily funded by local government contracts and grants from the local community foundation—they will receive a rating of "extreme." If they are largely funded by the same third-party payers but have some separate means, they will receive a rating of "high." If their funders are similar but not the same—for example, if they both rely heavily on grant funds but so far have tapped into different foundations—their rating will be "medium." Finally, if they use different kinds of third-party payers—for example, if one group relies on government funding and the other primarily earns its rev-enues through fees—their rating on overlap of third-party payers will be "low." In our example, the two leadership programs receive substantial funding from the same local community foundation, but each also collects fees from its participants and receives other minor support from additional third parties, so their rating on overlap of third-party payers is "high."

Using these definitions, it is possible to come up with a rough approxima-tion of the degree of relatedness of two organizations. Completing the Organi-zational Relatedness Index, will provide any pair of organizations with a relatedness score ranging from 4 (all lows) to 16 (all highs). Roughly, organizations with scores of 11 or higher are highly related and so are potentially intense competitors or collaborators.

Organizational Relatedness and Competitive Challenges

Nonprofits in the same field with more or less the same customer base, as well as nonprofits in somewhat related fields with similar but not identical customer bases, are faced with a host of competitive challenges, particularly if they have the same geographic scope:

- Customers: They seek the same customers.
- Staff: They seek similarly qualified staff members from the same pool.

- Board: They seek potential board members who are interested in substantially the same cause.
- Volunteers: They seek volunteers from the same community.
- Private funding: They seek funds from the same private sources interested in their field.
- Public funding: They seek government contracts through the same RFP processes.
- Marketing: They seek public recognition as a leader for work in the same field.

The list goes on and on. As you can see, nonprofits compete for many resources. Organizations can be intense competitors without competing for customers at all. The nature of competitive relationships and their extent can vary tremendously from situation to situation.

Groups with high overlap or relatedness are natural competitors, unless they form an alliance—for example, in one of the following areas:

- Customers: to serve different needs of the same customer
- Staff: to jointly attract a pool of qualified candidates for open staff positions
- Board: to increase awareness of their issue, enlarging the pool of board candidates
- Funding: to develop collaborative responses to public or private funding opportunities
- Marketing: to develop a coordinated media or marketing campaign

One might assume that nonprofits with a high degree of relatedness in program services, populations served, geography, or third-party payers must choose once and for all how to interact with one another—either to compete intensely or to collaborate closely. Real life, however, is seldom as straightforward as this. Even nonprofits with an extremely high degree of relatedness—for example, two human service agencies serving the same inner-city neighborhood—may both collaborate and compete. They may compete intensely for individual donors or for the support of an influential community group but at the same time form a hiring pool for hourly employees, share on-call services among their physicians, share space, develop a common billing arrangement, or even form an alliance to stave off a shared competitive threat.

The bottom line is that the more closely related the organizations are—that is, the higher they score on the Organizational Relatedness Index—the more intensely they are likely to be involved with one another. These relationships can be competitive, collaborative, or both.

Strategic Alliances

Between the two extremes—a high degree of relatedness leading to intense competition or collaboration at one end of the continuum and relatively little relatedness leading to less intense competition or collaboration at the other end—lies the middle ground of strategic alliances. These relationships exhibit a wide variability, perhaps because nonprofits at the medium-intensity level of relatedness have less clearly drawn organizational mandates for engagement with one another and thus have a wider range of options.

Here is an example. Honolulu Theatre for Youth provides a variety of educational and entertaining productions for school children statewide, reaching over 100,000 kids yearly. HTY looks to build its public audience and name recognition in order to attract more high-end donors. The Honolulu Symphony and Hawaii Opera Theatre each believe their future includes providing music education for children, building public awareness, and seeding the next generation of patrons. The geographic overlap of the three groups is extreme. The traditional customers of all three are likely to have a high degree of overlap, and all three groups want to reach school children. These groups wisely have decided to coordinate their youth-oriented efforts, initially jointly staging a production of *Green Eggs and Ham* for over twenty thousand children. If they did not coordinate, they would, by default, decide to compete, knowing that with the limited resources available in their state, it is likely that one organization would ultimately win the market for support of child-oriented productions, while the others would lose. Of course, a very real risk of a competitive strategy in such a situation is that all competitors could fail, by dividing an already small pie into slices too small to provide sustenance to any party's efforts. A merger is neither likely nor necessary, but a strategic alliance to jointly provide an educational opera is the beginning of a forward-looking and helpful strategy.

The Organizational Relatedness Index offers a subjective analysis, but nonetheless it is a useful tool for framing a consideration of how to approach competitors. We will use it as part of our competitor analysis in Part Two.

Conclusion

In this chapter, the Nonprofit Strategy Matrix provides a way of looking at both collaborative and competitive strategies from the point of view of the intensity of the relationship. At any given time and in any given situation, either a collaborative or a competitive strategy may be most appropriate, but the level of intensity of that strategy may best be predicted by the relatedness of the two entities. The Organizational Relatedness Index provides an easy-to-use tool for gauging how closely two organizations are likely to be involved. In order to both compete and collaborate effectively and ethically, leading to greater mission accomplishment, a nonprofit's leaders need to approach their tasks with a clear appreciation for the external environment they face, a solid but flexible strategy, and the right mix of skills and tools. Part Two will focus on these tools.

PART TWO

ASSESSING YOUR COMPETITIVE POSITION

The goal of this introduction is to familiarize you with some of the tools and resources you will use to assess your market position. Part One presented the case for nonprofits using competitive strategies that are grounded in the organization's commitment to its mission; the demonstrated effectiveness of its programs; and the knowledge, based on feedback from stakeholders, that it is providing needed value. This is the basis of ethical competition—and the only way that nonprofits should compete.

Your organization's knowledge and understanding of its effectiveness and of the value it provides comes from knowing its stakeholders—people and institutions with an interest in its success—including customers, third-party payers, paid and unpaid staff, and others. You must know your stakeholders' characteristics, needs, and preferences. This information will help you to understand your market position—that is, where you stand relative to others competing for the same resources. Armed with this knowledge, you can develop competitive strategies.

Part Two consists of three chapters that build on one another, helping you to learn about your market position. First, in Chapter Four, you will develop a profile of your nonprofit, assessing its competitive advantages and disadvantages. To gain perspective on your organization, in Chapter Five you will compare what you have learned about your organization with what you know about your principal competitors. Finally, Chapter Six will help you put the pieces together to form a picture of your market position.

Market Position Is Critical to Achieving Your Mission

In Part Two, you will answer the essential question Where do we stand? With a solid understanding of your market position, you will then formulate your initial response to the questions What market position do we want, and How will we get there? You will determine how to strengthen your market position, and it will become clearer when and how to use competitive strategies to further your mission.

As you know all too well, resources are limited. Because the bottom line in the nonprofit sector is mission rather than money, resources should go to those who can most effectively use them—often organizations that have a strong market position. As we saw in Part One, these groups tend to be especially good at securing resources, a situation that makes them even stronger and, hence, better able to achieve their mission. It's a virtuous cycle, and you want to be part of it.

Market Research: Learning from Your Stakeholders

Your stakeholders have valuable information. Your task is to learn what they know. First and foremost, they are sources of information on how well your organization is meeting the needs of its customers. Stakeholders can provide crucial information about your nonprofit, its competitors, and its overall position in its market. Part Two shows you how to gather and analyze market information and how to use it to understand your position.

By now, you are saying, "That sounds great, but how do I get all this valuable information, and how much work is that going to take?" It's really pretty simple. The process starts by being in conversation with your stakeholders. This conversation is called market research. Asking questions is what market research is all about, and listening is the most important aspect of market research. As Jared Sparks put it, "When you talk, you repeat what you already know; when you listen, you often learn something" (Goodman, 1997).

Most organizations have some sense of their strengths and weaknesses and how they are perceived in their market. However, most don't have a clear enough picture. More important, few know how to make sense of this information and use it to identify needed actions. Market research provides an ongoing process for obtaining information from the full spectrum of stakeholders and assessing it in order to develop a sound understanding of the organization and its competitive advantages and disadvantages.

The point of market research is to learn about your customers. Having collected this information, it is possible to evaluate your current position and to develop strategies to strengthen it. While you may not compete directly for customers, you do compete for the resources to serve them. Thus, knowing both your customers and how best to meet their needs is a critical competitive advantage not only in attracting additional customers but also in securing third-party payers, potential board members, volunteers, staff, and other resources for your organization. The mission-focused nonprofit competes for these resources based on its ability to serve its customers.

I said it was pretty simple. Market research is as much an art as a science. Its main tools are

- An open, objective, and inquisitive mind
- A genuine desire to learn from others
- An understanding of what information is needed and where it can be found
- Questions that will lead to the desired information
- Good listening skills
- An ability to identify useful information from a myriad of data

If conducting market research is engaging in a conversation with stakeholders, then in this conversation your job is to figure out which questions to ask of whom and then to listen to the answers carefully and objectively. I cannot adequately stress this last word—*objectively*. Sometimes the responses you will get may be difficult to hear, especially when someone is unhappy with your programs. Remember Jim Collins's admonition: "You must confront the most brutal facts of your current reality" (2001, p. 86). Market research helps to uncover the facts, good, bad, and brutal. Remember, if you hear bad news early, there is still time to fix the problem. Whether it is third-party payers losing confidence, disaffected customers, or negative publicity, avoiding bad news is akin to putting your head in the sand: it doesn't change reality, and it inhibits your ability to respond.

Based on an analysis of the information you collect, you can identify your organization's current market position and compare it to where you want to be. You can then identify, develop, and implement strategies to move toward your desired market position. That is the whole point of competition: obtaining resources that move you toward your desired position in the market so you can do the most good.

The Research Process

Market research is an iterative process; that is, it should be ongoing, with each round building on previous information. The market is a living organism; needs, demands, and even stakeholders change. You must always be in listen-and-learn mode. This may sound overwhelming, but once you develop a solid foundation of knowledge about your stakeholders, market, and competitors, you will find that it is relatively easy to keep it up to date. Ongoing sensing of the market gives you a broad perspective on your field. Over time, it will enable you to identify opportunities to improve your organization's position.

Resources to Help You in Your Research

There are many resources available to help you conduct market research. Stakeholders are information sources themselves, but they can also serve as researchers. Internal stakeholders-staff, board, and volunteers-can be extra pairs of eyes and ears, extending your reach. They can give you multiple perspectives, which are essential to forming a full picture of the market.

Because internal stakeholders may have biases, such as allegiance to the organization, it is critical to engage external stakeholders as well. Customers are the best and generally the most readily accessible source of unbiased information on your organization's strengths, weaknesses, and effectiveness. Given the variety of feedback that a market research process can generate, the tough part of the job is to sift through it all with an open mind. Remember that a person's perception, even if incorrect, is a form of reality. In fact, customers' perceptions are in many ways more important than objective reality. If they didn't like the service, no matter how good it might be, it still failed; if they hated the show, no matter how celebrated the playwright, they may not come back next season. This is the true meaning of the old expression "the customer is always right"; it is true even when the customer is actually wrong.

In addition to current customers, your past customers are a great source of information. Do you ever wonder why they are no longer your customers? They may no longer need your programs, which could be testimony to your effectiveness; they may now prefer a competitor; they may substitute another service that they find more effective, convenient, or affordable; or there may have been a change in third-party funding, leaving them unable to afford or access your programs any longer. Whatever the reasons, market research can uncover why they are no longer customers.

Similarly, every nonprofit has potential customers. If you hope to grow or even to replace customers lost through attrition, you need to learn about your potential customers—including whose customers they are (if anyone's), why they are not your customers, and what might encourage them to become customers. Remember, past customers are also potential customers.

Market Research and the Discipline of the Market

Earlier, I discussed the danger of mission creep. The market research model I present here places your mission and customers front and center in your consideration.

This approach effectively imposes the discipline of the market that may otherwise be absent due to the nature of the nonprofit economic model. If you know how customers perceive your nonprofit and how you can better serve them, you may be better able explain their needs to third-party payers, helping you to resist the forces that impel a nonprofit toward mission creep.

Where to Start

Start your market research by conducting a brainstorming session with your staff, board members, and other volunteers in order to identify what you want to learn. Include not only management staff but those closest to your customers. This will be your market research team (see Chapter Four for more on how to select a market research team). Through this brainstorming process, you will formulate research questions. You will determine what information you already have and what you need to learn. As you assess and compare your organization and your competitors, you will develop an understanding of the market and of your position in it. You will learn about your nonprofit's strengths and weaknesses and where there may be opportunities to enhance your position, as well as where it may be threatened.

An important first step is to identify key internal stakeholders (staff, board, volunteers, and members, if you have any) and external stakeholders (third-party payers, civic leaders, the media, and so on). Also include collaborators and competitors. Competitors initially may not want to share their opinions or answer your questions but can usually be persuaded to do so if you offer to answer the same questions for them in return.

The questions that market research helps to answer fall into a few key categories, which are displayed in the following list with some suggestions for the types of questions to ask.

Customers

- Who are our customers (past, present, and potential)?
- What do our customers think of us?
- What do they need or demand from us? What will their needs or demands be in the future?

Other Stakeholders

- Who are our other stakeholders (for example, funders, media, the public at large)?
- Why are they important to us? What resources do they offer us?

- Why are we important to them? What do they need or demand of us?
- What do they think of us?

Other Organizations

- What other organizations are in our market?
- Are these competitors, collaborators, or both?
- What are their strengths and weaknesses?
- What are our comparative advantages and disadvantages?

Market Share, Position, and Trends

- What is our market? How do we define it? Do we define our market by geography, mission, programs, customer needs, or something else?
- What are key characteristics of our market?
- How big is our market, and what is our share?
- What is our position? Is our organization the leader? A newcomer? One of a pack?
- What are the past, present, and future trends in our market?
- What opportunities and threats are there?

Conclusion

Part Two takes you through a market research process. During the process, you will focus first on understanding the needs of your primary stakeholders and on assessing how well you are meeting those needs (Chapter Four). Next, you will compare your organization with your key competitors (Chapter 5). Then you will look at your nonprofit and your competitors as a whole and identify your market position (Chapter Six). Finally, you will see when competitive strategies may be useful in attracting resources or improving your market position.

CHAPTER FOUR

YOUR ORGANIZATION'S COMPETITIVE POSITION

The goal of this chapter is to provide a framework for assessing how well your nonprofit meets its customers' needs and to help you identify your organization's competitive advantages and disadvantages relative to its market. To assess your organization, you ask a series of questions and then seek the answers primarily by listening to your stakeholders.

The Market Research Team

First, form a market research team composed of key board members, senior managers, and other staff and volunteers who are in close contact with your customers. Carefully select members of this team for the attributes listed in the introduction to Part Two, such as willingness to learn from others, good listening skills, and especially an open mind. Board participation on the team will make it easier later on to get board acceptance of the results; management participation is essential, since their work will be affected by what you learn; and frontline staff members have an invaluable perspective, since they are in the most direct contact with customers on a daily basis. Work through the recommended process with the close involvement of this team. That way, learning will be spread throughout the organization, preparing the way for action.

The Market Research Process

There are four steps to developing a sound assessment of your organization's competitive advantages and disadvantages in the market. Exhibit 4.1 provides an overview of the process.

Step 1: What Is Your Market Focus?

Begin by identifying your market focus: what you do (program focus), where you do it (geographic focus), and for whom (customer focus).

Program Focus. Like most nonprofit leaders, you can probably sit down and immediately identify your programmatic focus somewhat generically. You may say that your organization is a theater company, a provider of services for homeless people, or an environmental advocacy organization. Starting with this broad

EXHIBIT 4.1. THE MARKET RESEARCH PROCESS.

Step 1: What is your market focus?

Define your market focus and review it for mission alignment.

Key Questions

- What programs do we provide?
- What geographic area do we serve?
- Who are our customers (past, current, and potential)?

Step 2: How well does your organization meet your customers' needs?

Compare your intended customers with your actual customers.

Key Questions

- How do our customers perceive us?
- How well are we meeting their needs?

Step 3: How will current and future trends affect your organization and stakeholders?

Identify trends in your market.

Key Questions

- What are the trends in our market?
- How do the trends affect both us and our customers?

Step 4: Create a profile of your organization

Put all the pieces together to create a profile of your organization. Use this profile to conduct a simple self-assessment.

Key Question

- Considering our programs, our ability to meet customer needs, and market trends, what are our competitive advantages and disadvantages?

definition, try to establish the limits of what you do. For example, if you identify as an environmental advocacy organization, do you focus on a single issue (for example, clean air, toxics, or protection of a single species) or multiple issues (for example, preserving the environment in California)?

Whatever your answer, ask yourself why this is so. Is it merely because that is what you have funding to engage in today, or is it because your current programs are in total alignment with your mission? Remember, your vision and your passion for the mission should drive your organization's focus, not today's grants. The point of this exercise is to eventually define what business (or businesses) you are in; this process can be helped by determining first what businesses you are not in. Use the market research team for this exercise, but also be sure to test your proposed program focus statement broadly with internal and external stakeholders. Remember, too, that this is where you are today; in the future, your program mix may change as you find more effective ways of advancing your mission. Define your program focus reasonably—not so widely that any activity fits (which would render it useless) but not so narrowly that you have no room to consider new options or approaches as they arise. Here are some program focus statements from real organizations:

- We advocate for clean air at the state and local level by organizing grassroots constituents.
- We provide a range of school-based mental health services for children and families.
- We commission and perform new choral music for treble voices, providing children with an outstanding musical education experience.

Geographic Focus. Are you a local organization serving a neighborhood, city, or county? Or are you a global nonprofit based in the United States but working abroad? As with program focus, start by defining your geography as you normally would. Specify "We work here," but do not stop at this point. If you provide music education to local schools and a neighboring school district were to ask for your help, would your mission prevent you from responding positively, or would it encourage you? Again, push the limits in your questioning. Perhaps you would say yes to the neighboring school district, but what if a school district in another state then asked for your help?

Geography is a tricky component of market focus because everyone tends to define terms such as *local* or *regional* differently. Be sure to establish your geographic scope through an inclusive process similar to the one you used for programmatic focus. There are risks and opportunities with every geographic decision, and it determines to a large degree whom you will see as your competitors, so be sure to give serious consideration to this factor. Again, here are some examples of geographic focus statements from actual organizations:

- The focus of our work is California.
- We work countywide but are open to working in the neighboring county as well.
- We serve children from throughout the East Bay, but we tour and perform internationally.

Customer Focus. Customer focus is the most complex of the three factors included in market focus, so you will spend the most time on it. In seeking to better understand your past, current, and potential customers, you will need to enlist your market research team and additional internal stakeholders: staff, board members, and volunteers. Your customer research will be closely linked to the programmatic and geographic focus decisions you have made. Table 4.1 provides a framework for looking at programmatic, geographic, and customer factors together. If other customer features are important to your situation, add them to Worksheet 4.1 in Step 2, later in the chapter. Use Table 4.1, which describes the information needed in each section of the worksheet, as a reference, but write the information on Worksheet 4.1.

Getting Answers: Using Existing Data. To find the answers to your questions about actual customers, look first to existing information you maintain as part of your operations. This includes data on past and current customers and the programs they use. If yours is a membership organization, you probably have a database on members, your primary customers. If you have government contracts, financial and programmatic reporting requirements imposed by your third-party payers probably mean that you have fairly easy access to at least some needed information. Also look to customer comments that you may collect through internal quality control surveys or a "suggestion box."

You may be surprised to find that you don't have much data on your current customers. In this case, brainstorm with your market research team to capture the information you do have. Draw on your observations of customers. While this information is, admittedly, subjective, it is a reasonable starting point. If nothing else, this exercise will make you more aware of the need for customer data, which in itself is a positive outcome. Over time, you can develop simple processes to capture information that will help you better understand those you serve.

If your organization has collected data for the past few years, you can assemble and examine it chronologically to determine whether there are any notable trends.

TABLE 4.1. CUSTOMER PROFILE FRAMEWORK.

Mission: Write your mission statement. As you complete the table, evaluate your organization (for example, customers served) in the context of your mission.

Characteristic	Intended Customers (Target Market)	Actual Customers (Include any notable trends)
Customer needs	What customer needs are our programs intended to meet?	What customer needs do our programs actually meet?
Programs: How do we meet our customers' needs?	What programs do we offer?	Which of our programs do our customers use?
Geographic area targeted and served	What geographic areas do we seek to serve (for example, what neighborhoods, cities, regions, states)?	Where do our customers actually live and work?
Demographics of customers		
Age	What age groups are our programs intended to serve?	What age groups are our customers in?
Gender	Do our programs target women (or girls), men (or boys), or both genders?	What is the distribution of our customers by gender?
Socioeconomic status	Do we target potential customers in specific socioeconomic categories? How do we define these categories?	What is the distribution of our customers by socioeconomic status?
Languages spoken	What languages do our intended customers speak?	What languages do our customers speak?
Size of customer market	How many potential customers are in our target markets?	How many customers do we serve? What is our market share?
Capacity	How many customers can we serve? How much of the need can we meet?	What percentage of our capacity are we currently operating at, on average?
Payment for services	How do we expect that our customers will pay for our programs? (for example, self-pay entirely, self-pay subsidized, third-party payer only)	How do our customers pay for the programs they use? (Include distribution by type or source of payment.)
Access to programs	How do we make our programs accessible to our customers?	How do our customers access our programs (for example, during what hours, at which locations, using which types of transportation)?

(Continued)

TABLE 4.1. CUSTOMER PROFILE FRAMEWORK (*CONTINUED*).

Characteristic	Intended Customers (Target Market)	Actual Customers (Include any notable trends)
Communication	How do we help potential customers learn about us? What communication methods do we use?	How do our customers learn about our programs?
What barriers do our customers face in accessing our programs?	What barriers to access do we think there might be? What have we done to address these barriers and to make our programs accessible?	What barriers are there? (for example, lack of funding, safety concerns, lack of transportation, language barriers, inconvenient service hours)
Customer satisfaction	How do we expect customers to think of our programs?	How satisfied are customers with our programs?
Outcomes	What outcomes do we expect our customers to realize from us?	What outcomes do our customers realize?

A good rule of thumb is to look over the past three years. Examples of trends to look for include the following:

- Changes in customer composition (for example, changes in the number of customers, their ages, or location of their residence)
- Changes in service usage and length of involvement
- Changes in satisfaction levels
- Changes in source, rate, or level of payment by either customers or third-party payers

Getting Answers: Doing Survey Research. If you lack current customer data, consider conducting basic survey research to answer your questions. The best way to find answers is, obviously, to ask your customers themselves. To do this, design a simple survey. The emphasis here is on *simple*. Too complex or long of an instrument will cause errors and a low return rate, so stick to gathering the most essential data.

Ideally, your survey should have just five to seven questions, the majority of which should be closed-ended in nature. This means that someone can check off a response rather than having to write in an answer. Such surveys can be easily analyzed. Also, if the survey is given at periodic intervals, responses can be tracked over time for trends. (This is what professional polling firms do.) Of course, open-ended or essay-type questions usually elicit richer information, allowing you to identify critical nuances that you might otherwise miss. This benefit must be balanced against the challenge of getting people to participate and the greater difficulty of analyzing their responses.

In developing a survey, be aware of and accommodate any special customer needs; consider language, reading level, physical limitations, and other characteristics that will affect customers' ability to complete the survey. Often the best way to survey your customers is through an in-person or phone interview or through focus groups. This is a more time-consuming approach, but it allows you to ask follow-up questions to clarify ambiguities. Also, live survey methods help you to get responses that are more truly representative of customers than those obtained through written surveys, which often attract a disproportionate number of responses from people who are outliers—either very satisfied or very dissatisfied. A live survey can also be used to follow-up a mail survey, to probe in more depth, or to test new program ideas that arise from an earlier mail survey.

If you opt for a live survey, bear in mind that customers may not be as candid with a staff member as they would be with an outside researcher. Politeness or fear of retribution may cause people to hold back. An outside researcher can also ensure that responses will be confidential. For these reasons, it may be best to enlist the help of a college student or community member to conduct interviews. One last caveat: always test a survey before sending it out. Inevitably, there will be questions that are crystal clear to you but are confusing to outsiders. Try the survey on several civilians—spouses, friends, and coworkers—before finalizing it.

The primary questions that the survey should aim to answer include the following:

- Who are our customers? (basic demographics such as age, gender, and socioeconomic status)
- What geographic areas do we serve? Where do our customers come from?
- Which of our programs do our customers use the most? Why?
- Why don't they use other programs that we offer? (if applicable)
- How do our customers learn about our organization and its activities?
- What do our customers like and not like about us? What do we do well or poorly?
- How do our customers access us and what barriers inhibit them? (for example, transportation, cost)
- Why aren't past customers participating in our programs any more? Whose activities are past customers participating in now? Who are our competitors? Why?

Exhibit 4.2 provides a sample survey. This survey shows the types of questions that are most important to ask your customers. It is designed to be a mail survey

EXHIBIT 4.2. SAMPLE CUSTOMER SURVEY.

This survey is being conducted on behalf of ABC Organization. ABC would like to know your thoughts about its programs. Please answer the following questions. Your responses are confidential; no information identifying you will be made available to ABC. Your answers will help ABC to better understand the needs of its customers and to know where changes in its programs may be needed.

1. How did you learn about ABC? (Check all that apply.)
   _____ Advertisement/brochure
   _____ Friend
   _____ Family member
   _____ *(List other choices as applicable for your organization)*
   _____ Other (specify): _____

2. Which of the following services of ABC have you used in the past six months?[a] (Check all that apply.)
   _____ Service A   _____ Service B   _____ Service C
   _____ Service D
   _____ Other (specify): _____

3. Overall, how satisfied are you with the services of ABC that you have used in the past six months?[a] (Check only one.)
   _____ Very satisfied
   _____ Satisfied
   _____ Neither satisfied nor dissatisfied
   _____ Dissatisfied
   _____ Very dissatisfied

   If you answered "dissatisfied" or "very dissatisfied," please tell us why: _____
   _____

4. Are there any changes you would like ABC to make to better serve you? Please explain: _____
   _____

5. Would you recommend ABC to a friend or family member? _____ Yes
   _____ Maybe   _____ No. If you answered no, please tell us why not: _____
   _____

---

[a]Use a timeframe that will ensure that respondents are not commenting on experiences that are in the past and that are no longer relevant. This also ensures that all respondents are commenting on the same timeframe. Generally, this timeframe should not be older than the past year.

EXHIBIT 4.2. (*CONTINUED*).

6. Please tell us about yourself:

Age (Check one) (*use relevant categories.*)	Gender	What city (*or what zip code*) do you live in?	What is the total income of your houshold?	What is your race/ethnicity?	What is the primary language spoken in your household?
———— 20–29 ———— 30–39 ———— 40–49 ———— 50–59 ———— 60–64 ———— 65+	———— Male ———— Female	*(Have respondent fill in or create a list with check-off items.)*	*(Ask only if relevant. Use categories that are relevant for your customer population.)*	*(Ask if relevant for your organization and its services.)*	*(Ask if relevant for your organization and its services.)*

7. Please tell us any other comments about ABC Organization that will help it to better serve its customers. ————————————————
   ————————————————————————————
   ————————————————————————————
   ————————————————————————————

Thank you for participating in this survey. Please return your completed survey in the enclosed pre-stamped and addressed envelope. If you have questions about this survey, please contact ———————— *(contact's name)* at *(area code) XXX–XXXX.*

---

but can easily be adapted to be administered by phone or in person. In addition to helping you identify areas where you might improve your programs, a survey will elicit information on what you are doing well. You can use this information in your marketing messages. The fact that you conduct customer research is itself a competitive advantage, demonstrating that you are concerned about your customers.

As you can see, the questions in Exhibit 4.2 elicit information not only about your organization, but also about your competitors, which will be useful in Chapter Five.

Assessing Outcomes. The results of a nonprofit's programs, as opposed to the number of people who participated or its level of effort, are its outcomes. Children learning to read, a forest saved, a civil rights law passed, or other similar end results are of critical importance to your positioning with customers and other stakeholders, including third-party payers. When you survey customers, be sure to ask how your programs help them or otherwise produce a change they desire, not just what they think of your programs. Their responses will yield information that will be useful in promoting your organization. And of course, customer feedback will probably reveal areas in which your organization needs to improve its performance. Get to work!

Asking Questions Tells Customers You Care. In addition to helping your organization to evaluate itself, market research tells your customers that you care about
them and their opinions. This can go a long way toward strengthening your
relationships with them. Be sure also to thank them for providing feedback and to
let them know how the information they provide will be used. Finally, it is
important throughout this process to preserve customers' confidentiality.

Summary Market Focus Statement. Now that you have specified your program
focus, geographic focus, and customer focus, put it all together and describe
your market focus. Here are some examples:

- We provide mental health counseling for emotionally disturbed children
  between the ages of 5 and 12 living in Alameda County.
- We stage new dramas by up-and-coming playwrights from around the world
  for an audience primarily composed of highly educated young professionals
  living in New York City.
- With the support of key legislators, environmental activists, philanthropic foundations, and the general public, we advocate at the state level for legislation that
  will enhance the quality of the environment.

These simple statements define what you do, where you do it, and for whom.
They are powerful adjuncts to a mission statement and pave the way for market-
focused competitive strategies.

Step 2: How Well Does Your Organization Meet Your Customers' Needs?

Table 4.1 has a column for information on *intended customers*—those whom your
organization seeks to serve—and one for information on *actual customers*—those
who, for whatever reason, you actually do serve. Occasionally, these groups
coincide completely, but usually there is some degree of discrepancy between the
two. The size and nature of this gap is instructive, so be sure that the market
research team spends some time discussing it. See Chapter Seven for more on
strategies related to this situation.

Worksheet 4.1 is designed to keep your mission front and center, so start by
writing your mission in the space at the top. Don't get bogged down by trying to
answer every question fully on the first pass. Over time, as you develop your market research function, you can expand on the information, adding more details.
In completing the table, you will also identify which essential information is not
immediately available; you can then look for ways to obtain it, such as survey
research, which I just discussed. Remember, too, that even the information you
do have might be out of date, incomplete, or biased. So always remember to

WORKSHEET 4.1. CUSTOMER PROFILE.

Mission:_____

Characteristic	Intended Customers	Actual Customers	Discrepancies in Intended vs. Actual Customers	Ways to Address Discrepancies (including "do nothing" if actual customers are more consistent with mission)
Customer needs: What needs do we seek to meet?				
Programs: How do we seek to meet customers' needs?				
Geographic area targeted and served				
Demographics				
Age				
Gender				
Socioeconomic status				
Languages spoken				
Size of customer market				
Capacity				
Payment for services				
Access to programs				

(Continued)

Play to Win by David La Piana, ISBN 0-7879-6813-7, cloth, copyright © 2005 Jossey-Bass, An Imprint of Wiley.

WORKSHEET 4.1. CUSTOMER PROFILE (*CONTINUED*).

Characteristic	Intended Customers	Actual Customers	Discrepancies in Intended vs. Actual Customers	Ways to Address Discrepancies (including "do nothing" if actual customers are more consistent with mission)
Communication				
What barriers do our customers face in accessing our programs?				
Customer satisfaction: How do we expect customers to think of our programs? How satisfied are customers with our programs?				
Outcomes: How are we doing? What impact are we having? Are customers satisfied with our programs? Are other organizations serving our target customers?				
Other characteristics: *Add other characteristics that are relevant to your organization's programs or customers.*				

challenge your assumptions and test them widely. If you have multiple programs that serve different populations, perhaps even within different geographic areas, you may need to develop a separate profile for each.

Note that the "Intended Customers" column asks for more of a philosophical and values-driven discussion about what your organization intends to do, while the "Actual Customers" column requires an objective look at what you actually do.

Compare the "Intended Customers" and "Actual Customers" columns of Worksheet 4.1. What can be learned from gaps between intended customers and actual customers? Use the last two columns of Worksheet 4.1 to note the discrepancies between intended and actual customers and to identify how you might address those gaps. Be open-minded. For example, you may find that your actual customers are a better target market than your intended customers. You may learn about barriers to access for your intended customers that you were unaware of, or conversely, you may find that your marketing simply attracts the wrong customers.

For example, if you consider your primary customer base to be low-income persons in your community who need counseling, but your market research reveals that you are serving a large number of people in middle-income and higher-income brackets, you need to understand the reasons for this divergence. Why aren't your intended customers using your programs? Also, why are unintended customers using them? Is it location, the makeup of your staff, financial considerations, or something else? Internal stakeholders are key to answering these questions. Brainstorm with staff, board, and volunteers.

The next step is to seek out intended but unserved customers. Questions can be posed through focus groups or other survey research methods. A short survey can ask a sample of people from the target customer base a few simple questions. The objective is to learn the answers to the following questions:

- Are they aware of our organization?
- What do they know about it?
- What perceptions do they have of our organization and its programs?
- Which programs—from which organizations—do they use instead? Why?
- What might prompt them to use our programs? Are there any barriers to access?

This information can help you to determine whom you need to attract and how this might be done. You may decide to solidify your actual customer base, increasing your market share with this group, rather than try to attract other customers such as the ones you originally intended to serve. Viewed in this light, the situation could be an opportunity rather than a problem.

Step 3: How Will Current and Future Trends Affect Your Organization and Stakeholders?

As you collect and analyze customer and other market information over time, you will gain an awareness of your organization's market position—where you stand relative to competitors. (I will have much more to say about this concept in the following chapters.) You will also be able to track your customers' satisfaction with your programs, as well as changes in their needs.

Trend Analysis. Once your organization has a clear sense of its customers—current and potential, intended and unintended—you can research the trends affecting your customer base and, in turn, your market share—the portion of total possible customers that you currently serve. You may want to understand economic trends and public policy or funding developments that may affect demand for your programs. We know, for example, that increased unemployment in a community leads quite directly to increased rates of child abuse. Thus, unemployment trend data is critically important for child protection organizations. The overall objective of trend analysis is to assess whether your overall customer base or some portions of it are growing, stable, or declining and whether conditions will make one or another situation more likely in the future. Much of this information can be gleaned from readily available sources of economic and demographic data on the Internet.

In addition to keeping current on customers' needs, you should keep abreast of trends in your field. Read the relevant news; keep abreast of developments that affect customers and stakeholders; network with colleagues in your field; join professional and civic organizations. The information obtained and the relationships you develop through these efforts will help you to gain a better understanding of your market position and to develop effective strategies for strengthening it. This is as true for a national organization as for a narrowly local one. The most effective nonprofit leaders I know are those with strong peer networks and many sources of information.

Conducting Market Research on a Limited Budget. Having been in your shoes as an executive director for many years and through my experiences as a consultant to many nonprofit organizations, I know all too well the very real limitations on time and other resources available for market research. The approach I am recommending here acknowledges these constraints. I suggest that, in conducting research on market trends, you look for readily available information from Web sites of similar organizations or of associations representing your field or from a local Chamber of Commerce. The point is to obtain valid data and a context for your organization so that you can discuss your position in the market.

Highly complex original research is not necessary. Just find as much information as you can easily make use of in order to learn about your nonprofit and your
competitors.

Making Sense of Market Trends. There are two major market trends that you
must monitor: trends in need for your organization's programs and trends in funding that creates demand by paying for those programs. In order to remain
responsive as well as solvent, you need to determine whether your customer base
and available funding will increase, decrease, or stay the same in the future.
Remember that demand is not the same as need. Millions in Africa need anti-
retroviral drugs to live with HIV infection, but the demand on organizations providing these drugs is limited because of financial and political considerations. In
other words, when there is only enough money to serve a fraction of a larger need,
you have an artificially limited demand. You care about your constituents'
needs, but you can only respond programmatically to demand, which can be
defined as need plus money.

Review demographic, economic, funding, and other related data and trends,
and complete Worksheet 4.2. Once individual trends have been identified, summarize them to gain a picture of the overall impact and duration of these market trends on your organization.

Step 4: Create a Profile of Your Organization

The next step is to create a profile of your organization, drawing on what you've
learned about your organization so far in this process. This will be a useful reference throughout your market research efforts. Complete Worksheet 4.3, taking
into consideration what you've learned about your customers and potential customers and about the trends that may affect your organization in the short term
and longer term. The profile you will create in Worksheet 4.3 is oriented to helping you discover your organization's market position, its competitive advantages
and disadvantages as they relate to this market position, and the trends that
may affect this position.

First, fill in your responses to the middle column titled "Our Organization."
I describe how to complete the "Assessment" section (the columns on the right)
below.

After you have completed the "Our Organization" column, your final step is
to assess your competitive advantages and disadvantages. Note that this is only
a first pass on this task; you cannot really be confident of your assessment until
you have analyzed your key competitors, which we will do in the next chapter.
Complete the three columns under "Assessment." Based on your responses under

WORKSHEET 4.2. MARKET TRENDS AND THEIR IMPACT.

Factors Affecting Market Size	How This Affects Our Customer Base	Why We Believe This (rationale and sources of supporting data)
Demographics	According to demographic trends, the population we serve is _____ Growing _____ Stable _____ Shrinking	_____ The population is aging _____ The birth rate is increasing _____ Immigration to our service area _____ Emigration from our service area _____ Other (specify):_____
Economy	According to economic trends, the population we serve is _____ Growing _____ Stable _____ Shrinking	The economy is _____ Strong _____ Weak _____ Stable This results in _____ Increased/decreased need for our programs _____ Increased/decreased ability of our customers to afford our programs
Funding	According to funding trends, the population we serve is _____ Growing _____ Stable _____ Shrinking	Third-party payers' interest in and ability to fund our programs is _____ Increasing _____ Decreasing _____ Stable, unchanged
Political climate	As a result of the political climate, the population we serve is _____ Growing _____ Stable _____ Shrinking	Policies promoted by political leaders will affect our programs as follows: _____ Increase need/demand _____ Decrease need/demand _____ Have no impact on need/demand
Overall impact of trends on need or demand	Taking into account demographic, economic, funding, and political trends, the population we serve is _____ Growing _____ Stable _____ Shrinking	The trends that most affect our customer base are:

Play to Win by David La Piana, ISBN 0-7879-6813-7, cloth, copyright © 2005 Jossey-Bass, An Imprint of Wiley.

WORKSHEET 4.2. (*CONTINUED*).

Factors Affecting Market Size	How This Affects Our Customer Base	Why We Believe This (rationale and sources of supporting data)
Overall impact of trends on available funding	Taking into account demographic, economic, funding, and political trends, funding for our programs is _____ Growing _____ Stable _____ Shrinking	The trends and factors that most affect available funding are:
Expected duration of trends	We expect the impact of these demographic, economic, funding, and political trends on our customer base to be _____ Long in duration _____ Short in duration _____ Of unknown duration	The trends that most affect our customer base are _____ Long-term _____ Short-term _____ Unstable or unpredictable because they are affected by other trends

WORKSHEET 4.3. ORGANIZATIONAL PROFILE.

Feature (Record your sources of information, for future reference.)	Our Organization (Information should be as complete as possible.)	Assessment		
		Strength	Needs Improvement	Comments
Mission statement and other key messages: For example, vision statement				
Target populations served: (Compare actual with target.)				
Date established				
Customers				
Reputation *Note: This is a subjective measure. Respond to this question with your general "gut" assessment of your organization reputation. Draw on your survey findings.*	Is your reputation: _____ Excellent _____ Good _____ Fair _____ Poor _____ Very Poor Comments:			
Market Share: Your general perception of your organization's position in the market. (This will be completed in more detail when the competitor profiles are completed; see Chapter Five.) Include future trends in need or demand for programs by type, geographic area, and trends in the demographics of the population in need.				
Members (if applicable): Number, type, recruitment strategies, costs, and benefits of membership				
Recent, planned, or anticipated changes in membership (Explain.)				
Programs offered and populations served				
Service A: Type of service, type of customer (description), number served,				

Play to Win by David La Piana, ISBN 0-7879-6813-7, cloth, copyright © 2005 Jossey-Bass, An Imprint of Wiley.

WORKSHEET 4.3. (*CONTINUED*).

Feature (Record your sources of information, for future reference.)	Our Organization (Information should be as complete as possible.)	Assessment		
		Strength	Needs Improve- ment	Comments
length of time services pro- vided (experience in this area), reputation of programs				
Service B: Type of service, type of customer (descrip- tion), number served, length of time services provided (experience in this area), reputation of programs				
Service X: Type of service, type of customer (descrip- tion), number served, length of time services provided (experience in this area), reputation of programs				
Recent, anticipated, or planned changes in programs or population served (Explain.)				
Sites: Location and capacity (if applicable)				
Recent, anticipated, or planned changes in sites or capacity (Explain.)				
Finance				
Financial stability and market share: Total revenue, total expenditures, net gain or loss, and so on; trends over time				
Price: Cost per activity or unit of service and availabil- ity of subsidies, sliding scale, and so on				

(Continued)

WORKSHEET 4.3. ORGANIZATIONAL PROFILE (*CONTINUED*).

Feature (Record your sources of information, for future reference.)	Our Organization (Information should be as complete as possible.)	Assessment		
		Strength	Needs Improvement	Comments
Diversity of funding: Sources and amount of funding				
Development: Staffing, strategies (as applicable: membership base, donors, corporate funding, foundations, fees, endowment and size of it, and so on)				
Recent, anticipated, or planned changes in funding, financial stability, fundraising capacity, and so on (Explain.)				
Leadership				
Executive director: Experience, length of time in field, length of time with organization, background, expertise, and so on				
Board of directors: Size of board, leadership (for example, key community or business leaders), background, skills, expertise, and so on				
Advisory or leadership council (if applicable): Leadership, background, skills, expertise				
Recent or potential changes in leadership (Explain.)				
Staffing: Skills and qualifications of staff; number of full-time and part-time staff by type; key staff positions and persons filling them; expertise				
Turnover, especially in top leadership positions				

WORKSHEET 4.3. (*CONTINUED*).

Feature (Record your sources of information, for future reference.)	Our Organization (Information should be as complete as possible.)	Assessment		
		Strength	Needs Improvement	Comments
Recent, anticipated, or planned changes in staffing or retention (Explain.)				
Volunteers: Number, type, recruitment or retention strategies				
Recent, anticipated, or planned changes affecting number, retention, and so on of volunteers (Explain.)				
Marketing or Public Relations				
Marketing messages and strategies: How does your organization present itself to its various stakeholders? What messages does it give? How are those messages delivered? (Review marketing material, Web sites, presentations, proposals, and so on.)				
Media or publicity: Strategies, effectiveness; for example, number of "mentions" in local press, industry publications, number of Web site visits				
Recent, anticipated, or planned changes in marketing and PR capacity, strategies, or tactics (Explain.)				
Other				
Quality: Includes features such as whether the organization is accredited and the qualifications of staff or service providers				

(Continued)

WORKSHEET 4.3. ORGANIZATIONAL PROFILE (*CONTINUED*).

Feature (Record your sources of information, for future reference.)	Our Organization (Information should be as complete as possible.)	Assessment		
		Strength	Needs Improve-ment	Comments
Recent, anticipated, or planned changes that might affect quality (Explain.)				
Special awards and other recognitions				
Partnerships or collabora-tions with other organiza-tions (Describe.)				
Planned expansion: Capital campaigns for new build-ings, new sites, new pro-gram or service offerings, and so on				
Other future plans				

"Our Organization," identify whether each area is a notable strength of your organization or whether it is an area in which your organization needs improvement. At this point, just check off one column or the other, then review the overall results with your market research team. This discussion should yield a good understanding of your organization as it relates to the market and its customers. Do not skimp on time for this discussion; it is where the learning will come from. Use the "Comments" column to note additional information uncovered or insights you have arrived at while completing this worksheet. Feel free to add pages in order to capture your complete answers.

In the next chapter, you will refine this assessment by comparing your organization with others competing for resources in your market. Based on your analysis of the competition, it is likely that you will want to come back and revise your assessment. This is to be expected; market research, as I said earlier, is an iterative process.

In Part Three, you will begin crafting competitive strategies. You will be most effective in doing this if you are clear about your organization's strengths and weaknesses and how they translate into competitive advantages and disadvantages. You will also determine which strengths to capitalize on as you develop your competitive strategies.

Conclusion

In this chapter, I presented a four-step model of market research that helped you to define your market focus and then learn from your customers and other stakeholders about your organization. The result was a profile of your organization that will help you to identify your competitive advantages and disadvantages in relation to your competitors.

CHAPTER FIVE

COMPETING WITH INDIVIDUAL ORGANIZATIONS

The goal of this chapter is to deepen your understanding of your organization's competitive advantages and disadvantages in relation to the organizations that compete with you. You will build on the research you did in Chapter Four, in which you began to develop a good understanding of your own organization's market position.

This chapter uses a similar research process, but this time it is designed to help you learn about your competitors. These are the organizations that you compete with for resources, including customers, funding, media attention, board members, staff, and volunteers.

This chapter will take you through the process of completing an organizational profile for each of your major competitors. By comparing these profiles to that of your own organization, you will identify your top competitors' competitive advantages and disadvantages in relation to you, and, in turn, you will refine your assessment of your own organization. The result will be an enhanced understanding of your nonprofit's market position.

Direct and Substitutable Competitors

Using the same research process as the one you used in the preceding chapter to learn about your customers, you can also learn a lot about your organization's competitors. You are developing a better understanding of which organizations provide programs that are the same as yours, similar to yours, substitutable for yours, or complementary to yours. In conducting your competitor research, be sure to include for-profit organizations as well as nonprofits. In some cases, it may make sense to include service units of government that provide similar or substitutable programs. Also, consider organizations that may enter your market in the near future but that are not currently active in it. These potential competitors include organizations that target other geographic areas (such as a contiguous county). Potential competitors also include organizations operating in the same geographic area that do not currently offer similar programs but may consider doing so in the future. By keeping up-to-date on trends in the field or community, you will be better able to recognize conditions that might be attractive to potential competitors, anticipate their moves, and respond appropriately. I discuss this in more detail in the sections that follow.

In doing your competitor assessment, it would be a mistake to focus only on direct competitors—those with the same market focus, doing similar work in the same geographic area. These are easily identifiable; you can probably recite most of their names from memory. This is a good place to start, but it is important to think more broadly about competitors, to include in your analysis organizations that compete for customers by offering substitutable programs as well as organizations that compete with you for other resources—such as board members, staff, volunteers, and funding. I refer to the first type as *substitutable competitors* and the second type as *indirect competitors*. Table 5.1 shows the three types of competitors: direct, substitutable, and indirect. I will discuss direct and substitutable competitors now and indirect competitors later in this chapter.

An example should help to clarify the distinction between direct and substitutable competitors. Let's call our nonprofit child care center Happy Tots. Happy Tots competes for customers (the parents who purchase child care services), so the

TABLE 5.1. TYPES OF COMPETITORS.

Direct Competitors	Substitutable Competitors	Indirect Competitors
Organizations with the same market focus; organizations that do what you do, within the same geographic area, for the same types of customers	Organizations that meet the same need that you do but in a different way	Organizations that do not compete with you for customers but do compete for other resources such as funding, board members, and staff

people who run Happy Tots need to know what other nonprofit child care providers serve the same age groups in its service area. They need to know how these other providers are different from Happy Tots, who their customers are, and how their customers differ from Happy Tots' customers—if they do indeed differ. These are Happy Tots' direct competitors. But the people at Happy Tots need to know a lot more. They need to find the answers to questions such as the following:

- What governmental child care programs (for example, those run by school districts) serve the same area as Happy Tots?
- What family day care or for-profit day care centers are located in the area?
- How prevalent is the use of nannies working out of parents' homes?
- How many stay-at-home parents are providing care for their own children?
- How popular are shared child care arrangements with other families?
- What child care resources outside the neighborhood are parents choosing?
- What employer-provided child care are parents using?

All of these child care providers are in essence competing with Happy Tots. The limited resource that is the focus of this competition is children needing care; anyone who is providing that care, in any way, is occupying space in the child care marketplace. Obviously, the simple definition of a direct competitor as someone who is doing the same work in the same geographic area is not adequate to encompass all of the alternatives just listed.

Direct competitors are other child care centers, which compete with Happy Tots based on price, location, quality, and amenities. Substitutable competitors offer other means of meeting parents' child care needs: they substitute some other form of care for Happy Tots' center-based child care approach. Centers such as Happy Tots serve just a part of the local market, and, complicating things further, local kids are served both within and outside of the immediate neighborhood. Parents who drive their children to child care centers near their work or to the homes of relatives or friends located outside the neighborhood are also choosing substitutable competitors—alternative ways to meet the same need.

Happy Tots competes with other child care centers, but it also competes with nannies and stay-at-home parents. To attract more customers, the staff at Happy Tots needs to understand the alternatives, the choices that parents make, and the parents themselves. With this understanding, the staff can articulate the advantages of using Happy Tots and communicate these to these child care decision makers. For example, depending on the competitive mix and the motivations of the child care decision maker, Happy Tots's advantages over other choices may be variously articulated as follows:

> "We have the nicest facility, located in the most convenient spot on the commute route." (emphasizes the advantages of quality and convenience)
>
> "We have the best adult-to-child ratio in the community." (emphasizes the advantages of quality and safety)
>
> "Nannies get sick, but our center is always open." (emphasizes the advantage of reliability)
>
> "Grandparents are no longer sitting around waiting to provide child care for little Tommy; they are taking cruises, playing tennis, or still working." (emphasizes the advantage of reliability)
>
> "We understand the needs of working parents; that's why we open early and stay open late." (emphasizes the advantage of flexible hours to meet varied schedules)

The concept of substitutable competitors requires you to think very broadly about how your customers' needs could be met by different means. It requires knowing your customers and potential customers well enough to recognize the type of program they might desire to participate in and to understand the qualities of that offering in terms of the values they seek in a provider.

Customers' varying concerns segment the target market. For Happy Tots, one market segment is single parents; this segment is probably interested in flexible hours of operation. If Happy Tots's hours do not meet the needs of working single parents, then this market segment won't be attracted. Another market segment might be stay-at-home parents for whom flexible hours is not an important feature. These parents are primarily interested in providing their children with a positive social and development experience. They will be most interested in the richness and quality of the program. Happy Tots will not be able to appeal to all market segments, but it must know which segments it is choosing to serve and what they expect from a child care resource. Porter (1996, p. 68) calls this the need for making trade-offs in establishing a sustainable strategy.

To further clarify this concept of substitutable competitors, here are some other examples of needs usually served by nonprofits and the substitutable services or alternative approaches that customers might choose:

- *Treatment of depression.* The customer may seek mental health counseling from a nonprofit clinic, or he may choose a private therapist, medication prescribed by his family physician, herbal remedies, an exercise regimen, or self-destructive courses such as heavy drinking or drug use (which psychiatrists call self-medication).

- *Love of symphonic music.* The customer may choose to attend the symphony, to drop in on a free concert in the park, or to buy a new home stereo system and CDs.
- *Need for exercise.* The customer may join a YMCA, or she may begin running the local trails, buy a home exercise machine, or take up tennis on city-owned courts.
- *Use of leisure time.* The customer may join a community recreation center, or he may choose to go to the zoo or the beach, take long walks, or go to the movies.
- *Concern over loss of civil rights.* The customer may join the ACLU, or she may instead join a single-issue group related to a specific concern or attend demonstrations organized through the Internet without affiliating with any group.

Each of these examples begins with a nonprofit offering to meet the need. Those nonprofits may have direct competitors—other nonprofits with the same market focus—but there are also other purchases and choices which can be substituted for their programs. It is important that you understand both your direct competitors and the substitutions your potential customers can make. This understanding will help you to market your programs in the most effective manner. For example, if you run a symphony that is losing customers to home audio equipment and CDs, how does it compete with that? You must understand what it is that keeps potential customers from coming out for live concerts. Is it cost, location, the need for babysitting, or some other factor or combination of factors? When you understand what you are up against, you can respond. If you determine that many of the symphony's potential customers work downtown but live in the suburbs and thus are reluctant to commute back on weekends for concerts, you might try concerts at lunchtime or on early workday evenings to attract these music lovers.

Clearly, future trends and anticipated innovations need to be incorporated into your analysis. It is possible, as in the example of the symphony above, that the biggest competitive threat comes not from other providers of the same service but from a new technology or one that is coming in the near future. Whether it is home exercise equipment, high-end audio equipment, or the Internet, innovations can threaten to grab market share away from all competitors by redefining the market and making some offerings of all current competitors obsolete.

Researching Your Competitors

Drawing on the information you have already gathered and some which is still to be collected (see the rest of this section), you can develop a profile of each of your key competitors. This exercise will help you better understand your organization's competitive advantages and disadvantages. In Part Three, you will use this information to identify strategies to take advantage of market opportunities and to address potential threats to your market position posed by competitors.

Worksheet 5.1 is similar to the form that you used in Chapter Four to create the profile of your organization, expanded to allow you to examine your organization in comparison to each of your key competitors. The main task of this chapter is to complete this worksheet for each of your major direct and substitutable competitors. You will then have a profile of each competitor that you will use to compare it with your organization.

There are many readily accessible sources of information on competitors. Look back to work you did in Chapter Four, in which you assessed your organization's performance from the perspective of your customers. Your customer research is likely to have identified information on your competitors, so make sure that you include this. Ask others about the reputation of your competitors. Encourage people to be as objective as possible in assessing the competition. You need to understand the basis of their assessments in order to evaluate them.

In addition to the information gleaned through surveys and discussions with customers, sources of information on competitors include the following:

- Competitors' Web sites, which often provide a wealth of information, including press releases, marketing materials, and newsletters; annual reports and financial information; white papers; mission and vision statements; service descriptions; lists of awards, funders, and staff and board members and their qualifications; volunteer recognition strategies; and information on accreditation and future plans (for example, capital campaigns).
- Newspaper and journal articles
- Web sites of organizations representing the field or subsector (useful for trend analyses)
- Reports from funders on topics such as the state of the sector or subsector in your community, trends in funding, grant awards, or findings from surveys
- Web sites providing information on nonprofits, such as GuideStar and the Web site of the National Charities Information Bureau
- Presentations made at conferences

WORKSHEET 5.1. COMPETITOR PROFILE.

Feature (Information on all variables for direct competitors should be as complete as possible. Record your sources of information, for future reference.)	Competitor Organization	Our Organization	Assessment of Our Organization Compared to Competitor		
			Advantage	Disadvantage	Comments
*Mission statement and other key messages: For example, vision statement					
Date established					
Type of organization: nonprofit, for-profit, government					
*Type of competitor: direct, substitutable, indirect					
Customers					
Market share: The organization's share (percentage) of total dollars spent on programs, by type and geographic area (based on available information; data may not be complete, but what is available allows an analysis of relative market position). Changes in market share over time can be tracked if historical reports are available.					
Market share can also be measured based on the number of customers served in the past year, by service type and by geographic area. In addition, the number of sites where programs are offered can serve as a comparative measure.					
An additional component of market share to consider is future trends in need or demand for services by type, by geographic area, and by trends in the					

WORKSHEET 5.1. (*CONTINUED*).

Feature (Information on all variables for direct competitors should be as complete as possible. Record your sources of information, for future reference.)	Competitor Organization	Our Organization	Assessment of Our Organization Compared to Competitor		
			Advantage	Disadvantage	Comments
demographics of the population in need.					
*Programs offered and populations served					
Service A: Type of service, type of customer (description), number served, length of time services provided (experience in this area), reputation of programs					
Service B: Type of service, type of customer (description), number served, length of time services provided (experience in this area), reputation of programs					
Service X: Type of service, type of customer (description), number served, length of time services provided (experience in this area), reputation of programs					
Sites: Location and capacity (if applicable)					
Changes in focus of programs (type) or service delivery (past, present, and planned future)					
Members (if applicable): Number, type, recruitment strategies, costs and benefits of membership					

(*Continued*)

Play to Win by David La Piana, ISBN 0-7879-6813-7, cloth, copyright © 2005 Jossey-Bass, An Imprint of Wiley.

WORKSHEET 5.1. COMPETITOR PROFILE (*CONTINUED*).

Feature (Information on all variables for direct competitors should be as complete as possible. Record your sources of information, for future reference.)	Competitor Organization	Our Organization	Assessment of Our Organization Compared to Competitor		
			Advantage	Disadvantage	Comments
Financial					
Financial stability and market share (based on publicly available information such as GuideStar reports): Total revenue, total expenditures, net gain or loss, and so on; trends over time (as available)					
Price: Cost per activity or unit of service; availability of subsidies; sliding scale; and so on					
Diversity of funding: Sources and amount of funding (according to financial and other available reports)					
Development: Staffing, strategies (for example, membership base, donors, corporate funding, foundations, fees, nature and size of endowment)					
Leadership					
Executive director: Experience, length of time in field, length of time with organization, background, expertise, and so on					
Board of directors: Size of board, leadership (for example, key community or business leaders), background, skills, expertise, and so on					

WORKSHEET 5.1. (*CONTINUED*).

Feature (Information on all variables for direct competitors should be as complete as possible. Record your sources of information, for future reference.)	Competitor Organization	Our Organization	Assessment of Our Organization Compared to Competitor		
			Advantage	Disadvantage	Comments
Advisory or leadership council (if applicable): Leadership, background, skills, expertise					
Staffing: Skills and qualifications of staff; number of full-time and part-time staff by type; key staff positions and persons filling them; expertise					
Turnover, especially in top leadership positions: Actual statistics may not be easy to obtain, but review of job listings and discussions with others in the field help you gauge turnover					
Volunteers: Number, type, recruitment and retention strategies					
Marketing or Public Relations					
*Marketing messages and strategies: How the organization presents itself, where it puts its emphasis, who its key stakeholders are, and so on (from marketing materials such as brochures, Web sites, ads, articles, press releases, public service announcements)					
*Media and publicity: Strategies, effectiveness					

(*Continued*)

Play to Win by David La Piana, ISBN 0-7879-6813-7, cloth, copyright © 2005 Jossey-Bass, An Imprint of Wiley.

WORKSHEET 5.1. COMPETITOR PROFILE (*CONTINUED*).

Feature (Information on all variables for direct competitors should be as complete as possible. Record your sources of information, for future reference.)	Competitor Organization	Our Organization	Assessment of Our Organization Compared to Competitor		
			Advantage	Disadvantage	Comments
Other					
Special awards and other recognition					
Partnerships or collaborations with other organizations					
*Planned expansion: For example, capital campaigns for new buildings or new sites; new program or service offerings					
*Other future plans					
*Quality: Includes features such as whether the organization is accredited and qualifications of staff or service providers, based on publicly available information, news articles, qualitative information obtained through interviews, and your organization's leaders' experience and knowledge of the community					

Overall assessment

Competitor's advantages and disadvantages:

Your organization's advantages and disadvantages:

Your organization's greatest relative strengths:

Your organization's greatest relative weaknesses:

Comments:

Note: Asterisk (*) indicates information to complete for substitutable competitors.

For example, the people at Happy Tots might want to look at local groups that coordinate and advocate for child care; organizations and publications that support working parents; and other less obvious sources of information—for example, the job bulletin board at the local supermarket, to see what parents are looking for in child care and to get a sense of how popular various alternatives to center-based child care are in the community.

In addition to the sources suggested above, reflect on your own experiences. Consider the following items: Who comes to the professional meetings you attend? Who else bids on the contracts you seek? Who else is funded by your government and foundation third-party payers? Which of your donors shows up on the donor lists of other similar organizations?

One of the best sources of information on both the identity and characteristics of your competitors is your professional network—the relationships you have with others in your community and in your field. I can't stress enough the importance of getting information from outside of your organization. The most effective leaders are in touch with the community they serve and are well connected with others in their field.

As you seek to understand your organization's competitive advantages and disadvantages in relation to its competitors, look beyond your immediate network of colleagues. Identify experts whom you can learn from, and connect with them through reading their publications and attending conferences where they speak. Seek model organizations and best practices that you can learn from. One writer aptly expressed this concept thus: "Go to the place where the thing you wish to know is native; your best teacher is there. . . . You acquire a language most readily in the country where it is spoken; you study mineralogy best among miners; and so with everything else."

One leader of a successful nonprofit recently shared her approach to market research with me. In addition to maintaining contact with her customers, she has developed an informal network of advisers. She uses this network to share ideas, keep tabs on emerging trends, and get feedback on possible strategies. She tries to always be open to new information and freely shares the information she has collected with others. While staff members of your organization's immediate competitors may not be willing to talk candidly with you, those in similar organizations in other geographic areas that do not view you as a competitor may be eager to exchange ideas. You can meet these people at national and regional conferences.

Creating Competitor Profiles

Worksheet 5.1, the Competitor Profile, should be completed for both direct and substitutable competitors. The most detailed information available will be for your

direct competitors. Again, this should include organizations that you can determine are likely to expand into your organization's market in addition to those that
are already there. Use all of the research tools described earlier—surveys, focus
groups, Internet research, professional contacts, and your staff's experiences—
to form the fullest possible picture of your competitors.

Less information may be available for substitutable competitors, but including them in the table will help you keeps them in mind. They allow your organization another point of comparison and may reveal your competitive advantages
and disadvantages from another perspective. While all categories of information
in the profile are relevant for direct competitors, those with asterisks are most
relevant for substitutable competitors.

The market research tool mentioned in the introduction to Part Two—an
open, objective, and inquisitive mind—is very important in assessing competitors.
It helps to counter the natural human tendency to distort, either favorably or
unfavorably, information about oneself. Above all, it is important to conduct this
research in an ethical manner. You seek information on competitors in order to
better serve your customers and your community. Information should not be used
to attempt to harm or undermine competitors, nor should a nonprofit leader ever
bad-mouth the competition. This is in poor taste and tends to rebound on the
trash-talker. The way you can compete and win is by developing and emphasizing your competitive advantages and minimizing your competitive disadvantages.

I have included a column for information about your organization in Worksheet 5.1. If your own organization is included, the resulting analysis will be more
comprehensive, yielding a fuller picture of your market and providing for easier
assessment of the position of all competitors. Essentially, this information is the
same as the profile you developed for your organization in Chapter Four.

After you have filled in the information about your own organization, create
an individual profile for each competitor. Each profile should have one column
for your organization and one for the competitor. Start by completing the first
column—the one for the competitor. Then add the information on your organization that you developed in Chapter Four by cutting and pasting it into the second
column.

Identifying the Competitive Advantages and Disadvantages of Your Competitors

After you complete the profile, you will compare and contrast your organization with the selected competitor and complete the columns under "Assessment" that summarize this comparison. You will identify whether the area

under consideration provides you with a competitive advantage over your competitor or a disadvantage. As you compare your organization with the competitor, consider whether your assessment of your organization needs to change. Earlier, you looked at your organization in isolation. Now you are comparing it with a competitor, which may lead you to see your nonprofit in a different light. Are there any areas where your organization looks less favorable? If so, take heart. One leader made this comment about competitors: "They inspire me to recognize my weakness. They also inspire me to perfect my imperfect nature."

Identifying Your Top Competitors

After you have completed your competitor profiles and determined the relative competitive advantages and disadvantages of your organization and your competitors in the individual areas profiled, select the top five direct competitors and the top three substitutable competitors, based on which ones cause you the greatest overall concern. These should be your strongest competitors.

Depending on the characteristics of your market, you may have more or fewer competitors than the number I suggest profiling. Make sure that you don't arbitrarily limit the list. You need to strike a balance in determining how many competitors to track. You don't want to lose sight of competitors that may not be a threat now but that may nonetheless have important competitive advantages that you should be aware of; on the other hand, tracking too many competitors could be overwhelming and would dilute your focus and, eventually, your strategies. So include all competitors that you consider notable. Even if you do not have a lot of information on an organization, if you believe that it is an important competitor (or that it may be in the future), create a profile with whatever information you have available on the organization. This process is iterative; your information will evolve over time as you learn more and refine your thinking about your competition and as you develop and implement your competitive strategies and assess their impact.

It is essential to avoid the mistake of becoming too focused on one competitor. This can happen for a variety of reasons, such as the competitor's high visibility, physical proximity, or the relationships—positive or negative—that you have with leaders of the competitor organization. While this competitor is probably very important to understand, too intense a focus on it alone can cause you to overlook other competitors and thus be unable to fully evaluate your own market position. For example, you may perceive your organization to be in a poor market position because of a much bigger and better-known competitor. This perception may be accurate. However, if you look at the market as a whole, you may find that being number two in a large and growing market is actually a pretty strong position.

Indirect (or Resource) Competitors

While your direct competitors and substitutable competitors should be the main focus of your research, there is another group you should not overlook: indirect competitors. While they do not have the same market focus and thus do not compete with you to meet the same needs of the same customers, they do compete for other resources. Specifically, they compete for

- Funds, whether from private foundations, government, corporations, donors, or members
- Human resources—skills and expertise of board members, other volunteers, and staff
- Media attention and the resulting visibility and awareness
- Community leaders—for example, as spokespersons and advocates

These are all tangible resources. They can also yield intangible value to organizations by virtue of the credibility they bestow. Many third-party payers, such as foundations, like to fund organizations that can demonstrate solid financial support from other sources. Strong boards attract additional strong board members, who lend credibility to an organization and heighten its stature among its stakeholders. Good leaders and skilled staffs help organizations recruit others, and also bring the organization better visibility. Volunteers spread positive comments about their experiences to their friends and relatives who may then support the organization because of their relationship with the volunteer. Positive media attention brings credibility and heightens an organization's standing in the community.

Let's assume that you are executive director of a regional performing arts presenter. You have learned from your competitor analysis that your major direct competitors are the local opera company and the regional repertory theater and that the people who historically have been performing arts patrons for all of you are increasingly just staying at home with high-end audiovisual equipment—a substitutable competitor of everyone in your field. So far, so good: you have learned about trends in your field and their impact on your market, and now you better understand why your customers and potential customers make the choices they do. This is good information, but it does not yet fully describe your competitive landscape.

Let's further assume that in your community, the big donors, corporate sponsorships, and media attention are attracted, along with the best board members, to the local branch of the Humane Society. You have always known this but have ignored the Humane Society because they are not in your field, so they are not a competitor. Wrong! In fact, the Humane Society may be a key indirect competitor of your organization and all others in your community. While it has a different market focus—it meets different needs and does not compete with you for customers—the Humane Society has developed a winning formula that attracts a disproportionate share of the resources that you too need.

You need to understand how the Humane Society attracts resources and why it appeals so strongly to its supporters, so that you can learn from its success and compete more effectively for the resources it now seems always to win. As an added incentive to undertake this effort, keep in mind that there is only so much room for marquee nonprofits in any community. If you can enhance your standing by learning from the Humane Society, so can your direct competitors. If any organization can break the Humane Society's lock on high-profile donors and media attention, it is important that it be yours.

Do not pass over this question lightly by saying, "Of course they get all the big supporters; they take care of poor, cute, helpless animals. We cannot compete with that." While subsector or field may play a large role in the success of the top nonprofits in your community, you can likely find other communities in which the Humane Society is not the most successful resource competitor. Serving an attractive cause such as children or pets gives an organization an advantage, but what it makes of that advantage—how much it derives from it—can still be instructive to you.

Examining the top nonprofits in your market or community—not just those in your subsector—can produce a more comprehensive picture of your market. Examination of indirect competitors who have successfully secured the kinds of resources that you also seek provides insights into the factors that make these organizations effective. Your organization can learn from its indirect competitors and may even be able to use them as models in developing its organizational capacity in areas such as marketing, communications, and media skills.

Worksheet 5.2, the Indirect Competitor Worksheet, should be completed based on the identification and review of indirect competitors who compete with your organization for noncustomer resources. The focus should be on the key resource areas in which they compete with your organization. Later, in Part Three, you will use this information to inform your competitive strategies.

WORKSHEET 5.2. INDIRECT COMPETITOR WORKSHEET.

Competitor's Name	Resources We Compete for	Their Advantages	Our Advantages	Comments (for example, what can we learn from this organization?)
1.				
2.				
3.				
4.				
5.				

Conclusion

Now that you have developed a good understanding of your organization's competitive advantages and disadvantages in relation to your direct, substitutable, and indirect competition, you are ready to put these individual pieces together to create a picture of your market and your position in it. This is the focus of Chapter Six.

CHAPTER SIX

BENCHMARKING AGAINST THE FIELD

In this chapter, I describe how you can draw on the work you have done so far to create a picture of your overall market and to identify your organization's position within it. Based on an understanding of your organization's market position and its competitive advantages and disadvantages, as well as an awareness of trends likely to affect your market, you will be able to identify the position you would like your organization to occupy and then determine when competitive strategies may be effective tools for moving in that direction.

By following the process outlined in this chapter, you will further develop your understanding of many dimensions of your market. You will focus on

- Your direct, substitutable, and indirect competitors
- The needs of your customers and other stakeholders
- How well you are meeting these needs

Based on this understanding, you can learn where you stand in relation to your market. You will be looking to answer questions such as

- Does your market have many competitors or just a few?
- Is your market growing or shrinking, in terms of both needs and available funding?
- What position do you occupy: the leader, one of many strong organizations, or a small fry?

- Are you a strong player positioned for market leadership or focused on a particular niche?

These are only a few of the possible questions, which give you a sense of the many possible combinations of market environment and your position. Once you create a composite of your competitors, your customers, and trends in your market, you will be able to determine where your organization is positioned. You will answer the question posed in the introduction to Part Two: Where do we stand? Remember, as in the previous chapters, it is essential to go through this process with your market research team. You cannot do this alone. A team approach keeps everyone focused on the big picture. It also keeps everyone honest where bad news is concerned. Perhaps most important, as the team goes through this process together, it learns together, setting the stage to quickly move from strategy formation to action.

The final section of this chapter provides a framework for you to identify where competitive strategies, as opposed to collaborative ones, may be of most use to your organization. This lays the groundwork for Part Three, which is about developing competitive strategies.

Analyzing the Competitive Marketplace

The starting point for determining your market position is the competitor profiles you developed in Chapter Five, in which you identified your top direct and substitutable competitors. After you have reviewed these profiles, identified your competitive advantages, and summarized strengths and weaknesses (at the bottom of the Worksheet 5.1), use Worksheet 6.1 to synthesize the information you have gathered on each of your major competitors. By arraying this information on one sheet for each competitor, you will begin to develop a picture of your overall market.

Worksheet 6.1 should be completed for each of your organization's top competitors as well as for other organizations that have a specific competitive advantage over your organization or over the market in general.

The first step is to calculate the Organizational Relatedness Index score for each major competitor, based on the degree of overlap in key features between you and the competitor (see Chapter Three). Record the total score and the areas of highest relatedness in the first column of Worksheet 6.1.

Now you are ready to identify the specific competitive advantages of each major competitor in relation to your organization. Rate each item in the "Key Performance Area" column. Is this item an area of strength for this

WORKSHEET 6.1. COMPETITOR ANALYSIS WORKSHEET: DIRECT COMPETITORS AND SUBSTITUTABLE COMPETITORS.

Competitor's Relatedness to Our Organization	Key Performance Area	Organization's Advantages and Disadvantages in Relation to Our Organization (check one for each attribute)			Comments (Why is this an advantage or disadvantage? What are the implications for our organization?)
		Advantage	Neutral	Disadvantage	
Competitor's name:	*Customers (overall)*				
	Satisfaction with programs				
	Reputation of organization				
Type of competitor:	Market share (large market share = advantage; small market share = disadvantage)				
___ Direct	*Program (overall)*				
___ Substitutable	Quality of programs				
Relatedness score: ___	Effectiveness of programs				
Areas of highest relatedness to our organization: (check if score is 3 or 4)	Strength of mission-focus				
	Finances (overall)				
___ Similarity of programs	Financial stability				
___ Overlap of customers	Funding diversity				
___ Overlap of geographic service area	Fundraising				
	Leadership/Human Resources (overall)				
___ Overlap of third-party payers	Board				
	Executive				
	Staff				
	Volunteers				
	Marketing/Communications/Public Relations (how effective, well known)				
	Other (add rows as needed)				
Overall assessment: How strong a competitor is this? (Write your comments here)					

Play to Win by David La Piana, ISBN 0-7879-6813-7, cloth, copyright © 2005 Jossey-Bass, An Imprint of Wiley.

competitor, translating into a competitive advantage? Or does the competitor perform poorly in this area, making it a competitive disadvantage?

A key purpose of this exercise is to learn about your market position by studying those of your competitors; if a competitor has an advantage, learn from it. As someone once said, "You can't destroy good ideas. Take advantage of them!" It can be hard to admit that someone else has a better program, but if your market research indicates this, you need to acknowledge it. If, for example, another advocacy organization has an excellent track record of successful legislative battles, while the reputation of your organization is mixed, it is time to face this brutal reality openly—and to learn from your competitor.

You have summarized all the key information you have collected about each competitor through your market research process. Now that you have completed Worksheet 6.1 for each of your top direct competitors and each of your top substitutable competitors, turn the tables and complete the worksheet for your own organization, considering how it stacks up against these competitors. Consider how customers perceive your organization, how satisfied they are with your programs, what value they place on your organization's work, and, ultimately, what they think of you. Is your overall reputation excellent, good, fair, or poor? This profile of your own organization will complete your picture of the players in your market and show how your organization fits in.

Worksheet 6.1 is designed to provide a snapshot of each competitor. Its main categories correspond to the primary resources in the market and include an assessment of your and your competitor's programs. These are the resources you compete for, the resources you need to accomplish your mission. In Part Three, I devote a separate chapter to various strategies that you can employ to secure these needed resources.

Determining Your Market Position

Now, using these assessments, complete Worksheet 6.2, which summarizes key information for all the major competitors in your market. Be sure to include your own organization, so that you can easily compare yourself with your competitors.

Once you have completed Worksheet 6.2, step back and look at where your competitors' advantages and disadvantages lie. Who is strongest in each of these areas? Is there an overall strongest competitor?

The next step is to develop a picture of the relative market position of each of your top competitors. You will need to consider the assessment of market share that you created as part of Worksheet 5.1. Remember, market share is the proportion of the total possible market that an organization can claim as customers.

WORKSHEET 6.2. MARKET SUMMARY: DIRECT COMPETITORS AND SUBSTITUTABLE COMPETITORS.

Relatedness to Our Organization

First competitor's name: _____
Relatedness score: _____
Areas of highest relatedness to our organization:
(check if score is 3 or 4)
_____ Similarity of programs
_____ Overlap of customers
_____ Overlap of geographic service area
_____ Overlap of third-party payers

Overall assessment: How strong a competitor is this?

Key Performance Area	Competitor's Advantages and Disadvantages (advantage = 1; neutral = 0; disadvantage = −1
Customers (overall)	
Program (overall)	
Leadership/Human Resources (overall)	
Finances (overall)	
Marketing/Communications/Public Relations	
Total (sum columns)	

Relatedness to Our Organization

Second competitor's name: _____
Relatedness score: _____
Areas of highest relatedness to our organization:
(check if score is 3 or 4)
_____ Similarity of programs
_____ Overlap of customers
_____ Overlap of geographic service area
_____ Overlap of third-party payers

Overall assessment: How strong a competitor is this?

Key Performance Area	Competitor's Advantages and Disadvantages (score)
Customers (overall)	
Program (overall)	
Leadership/Human Resources (overall)	
Finances (overall)	
Marketing/Communications/Public Relations	
Total (sum columns)	

Our organization's name: _____

Overall assessment: How strong a competitor is your organization?

Key Performance Area	Our Organization's Advantages and Disadvantages (score)
Customers (overall)	
Program (overall)	
Leadership/Human Resources (overall)	
Finances (overall)	
Marketing/Communications/Public Relations	
Total (sum columns)	

Play to Win by David La Piana, ISBN 0-7879-6813-7, cloth, copyright © 2005 Jossey-Bass, An Imprint of Wiley.

It is important to first define your total market. For example, if you operate a homeless shelter, how many homeless people are in your community? This information may be readily available from U.S. Census or other government data. On the other hand, if you are an advocacy organization defending the rights of immigrants, you might want to define the total market in terms of those willing to support your cause through a membership, or you might define it as the total philanthropic dollars available to support your cause. It is unlikely that you will define it as the total number of immigrants in need of help, unless your programs provide direct counseling and legal assistance. The point is to define your market clearly so that you can determine how much of a market exists and what part you and others currently serve.

One more consideration: in many markets, the total market share controlled by all competitors may be minuscule. For example, all the counseling centers in town may, together, serve only a small fraction of those in need of counseling. In this case, it may be more helpful to define the market in terms of demand (need plus funding) than purely in terms of need. For example, if local government provides funding for one thousand counseling clients per year and your market is dominated by this third-party payer, you might use this number as your total market.

If you narrow the definition of your market, however, keep in mind that you have defined your target market as only a small portion of the potential market, which could be expanded exponentially by changes in third-party payer policies, government policies, or funding levels. If governments around the world decided to provide anti-retroviral drugs to every HIV-positive person in Africa, demand for the programs of organizations that distribute these drugs, which is now artificially limited by inadequate funds, would explode. The need would not have changed one bit; only the demand created by the availability of additional funding to meet the need would change.

Which competitor has the largest market share and the largest number of competitive advantages? Enter this information in Worksheet 6.3. The Organizational Relatedness Index score and total "Advantage" score for each competitor can be found on Worksheet 6.2. The total "Advantage" score is the total from the "Competitor's Advantages and Disadvantages" column on Worksheet 6.2. Sort the competitors by market rank; start with the strongest competitor, and follow with the others in rank order. In the "Comments" column, explain why you assigned this rank. For example, an organization may have a small market share compared to others, but it may be considered a stronger competitor because of the excellence of its leadership, the effectiveness of its programs, or by the very fact of its smaller size, which makes it more nimble and better able to respond to a changing market. Also note any trends or upcoming changes (for example, new programs to

WORKSHEET 6.3. MARKET POSITION.

Market Position/Rank (1 = top competitor)	Name	Direct (D) or Substitutable (S)?	Organizational Relatedness Index Score	Relative Market Share (small, medium, large)	Total "Advantage" Score from Worksheet 6.2	Comments (including trends that may affect the organization's position)

Play to Win by David La Piana, ISBN 0-7879-6813-7, cloth, copyright © 2005 Jossey-Bass, An Imprint of Wiley.

be offered, expanded service delivery sites, new partnerships, changes in third-party payer policies, new leadership) that may affect a competitor's position in the future.

Market Niche

A market niche is a well-defined and delimited place in the market that is relatively easily defended. A nonprofit can compete for overall market share, trying ultimately to become a market leader by gaining broad acceptance or ubiquity, or it can define a unique niche that plays to its strengths that it will defend from others. Remember that in selecting a niche strategy you may be artificially limiting your market, so make such a decision carefully, basing it on a clear commitment to build a position on your organization's unique strengths. For example, several years ago, my clients at an Asian health center wisely decided that the center could not compete with the large, mainstream health system that dominated its market. They considered, reluctantly, letting the health system acquire their health center, until they determined that its unique cultural and linguistic capabilities suggested a natural niche position. Rather than allowing the health center to be acquired, they contracted with the health system and others to serve this population, creating a niche market position that is relatively safe, for the time being. Niche positioning is an alternative you should keep in mind throughout this process.

Indirect Competitors as Complementary Competitors

Next, consider your indirect competitors. Look back at Worksheet 5.2 and pick your top indirect competitors (also called resource competitors). Think of their competitive advantages in relation to your organization. Worksheet 6.4 asks you to expand on your summary analysis from Worksheet 5.2. Consider your indirect competitors' competitive advantages as they relate to the different resources that you compete for. First, simply check off the resources you believe this competitor competes with your organization for. This will provide a good overview of the breadth of competition you face, as well as its focus (for example, are you mostly competing for staff?). Then, in the column on the right, draw on any information previously gleaned from your market research efforts, and other knowledge you may have of the competitor, to rate the competitor relative to your organization.

There are two primary reasons for considering indirect competitors in your strategy development process. First, they may have competitive advantages that your organization can learn from. For example, if another nonprofit is always in your community's news, garnering significant positive press, while your

WORKSHEET 6.4. INDIRECT COMPETITORS.

Competitor's Name

First competitor's name: _____

Resources We Compete for

Human	Board	
	Executive	
	Staff	
	Volunteers	
Funding	Foundations	
	Major Donors	
	Corporate Donors	
	Government Contracts	
Awareness	Media	
	Public at Large	

Attribute/Area	Competitor's Advantages and Disadvantages (advantage = 1; neutral = 0; disadvantage = −1)
Overall reputation	
Customer satisfaction	
Leadership/Human Resources (overall)	
Finances (overall)	
Marketing/Communications/Public Relations	
Total (sum columns)	

Competitor's Name

Second competitor's name: _____

Resources We Compete for

Human	Board	
	Executive	
	Staff	
	Volunteers	
Funding	Foundations	
	Major Donors	
	Corporate Donors	
	Government Contracts	
Awareness	Media	
	Public at Large	

Attribute/Area	Competitor's Advantages and Disadvantages (advantage = 1; neutral = 0; disadvantage = −1)
Overall reputation	
Customer satisfaction	
Leadership/Human Resources (overall)	
Finances (overall)	
Marketing/Communications/Public Relations	
Total (sum columns)	

Play to Win by David La Piana, ISBN 0-7879-6813-7, cloth, copyright © 2005 Jossey-Bass, An Imprint of Wiley.

organization struggles to get media attention, perhaps you can learn from their success. How do they get such great coverage? Is it simply that they are, like the Humane Society, in a sexier field, or is there something they do to attract all the attention they receive?

The other reason to keep indirect competitors on the radar screen is that they are very real competitors. While they provide different programs than you do, perhaps for entirely different constituents, they may nevertheless be attracting top-notch board members, dedicated volunteers, first-rate staff, or other resources that you would also like to attract. In Part Three, I discuss in more detail the challenge of competing with indirect competitors for resources.

Putting It All Together

Now that you have completed the first round of your market research process, it is time to synthesize all the information you have gathered into an understanding of your market position. You have identified your top competitors and collected a fair amount of information on them. The worksheets provide a format for this analysis, but the conclusions your market research team draws, as well as the actions your organization decides to take as a result, must come from a careful consideration of all your knowledge of and experience with your market. This is not by any means a rote process. Through this process, you will turn all the raw information you have collected on customers, market trends, and competitors into an understanding of the major dynamics of your market.

For example, you might learn that most of your direct competition comes from a branch of local government or that you are at a real competitive disadvantage because many of your direct competitors boast a nicer facility that appeals to customers. It might be important to learn that your organization's major (or only) competitive advantage is that its programs are the least expensive in town (low-price leadership). These bits of market intelligence, if they emerge, will help you to develop a better understanding of your current competitive position. Turning market information into intelligence is the result of analysis and interpretation. It is hard work, and there is no way around it.

How does an organization analyze all of the quantitative and qualitative data that have been gathered on its market and competition? Kearns (2000) cites a variety of portfolio analysis matrices that researchers have developed to assist decision makers in determining their best course of action. Portfolio analysis considers the range of an organization's activities—its portfolio. Kearns concludes that "portfolio analysis is most valuable when it is used as a heuristic device, not as a cookbook for strategy development" (p. 128). In other words, one cannot expect, simply by following the steps of any portfolio analysis process, to emerge at the end with a clear set of strategic initiatives. There are too many different dimensions along which competitors can be compared, making it impossible to fit them into a single matrix. Moreover, the importance of any one dimension will vary, based on the priorities and market realities of the organization that is conducting the analysis.

Portfolio analysis techniques help to surface issues for discussion (incidentally, that is what Kearns' term *heuristic* refers to) and may lead to insights by identifying what is most important for you to consider in developing strategies. However, these techniques are no substitute for careful thought, discussion, and debate among your organization's leaders.

The Market Position and Strategy Matrix

I will not attempt to develop yet another model of program portfolio analysis here. All such models, although they can be useful, ultimately try to reduce complex political, philosophical, financial, and cultural business decisions to a search for the correct box on a matrix that will reveal the best course of action. Instead, by drawing on several models, I have developed the Market Position and Strategy Matrix, shown in Table 6.1. This matrix summarizes key aspects of competitive position, market trends, and competitive dynamics, and suggests possible strategies for any given set of circumstances in your market. Because of the three-dimensional nature of competitive position, number of competitors, and market trends, the table represents many possible combinations. It is not intended to dictate strategy (You should distrust any process that does!) but rather to generate and focus discussion about strategy in your organization.

Market Trends. A market can be characterized as (1) growing, (2) shrinking, or (3) stable or stagnant (not significantly growing or shrinking). When you consider your market in these terms, look ahead to the next two to three years and consider two aspects of growth: our old friends need and demand. Is the need for your organization's programs or activities growing, staying about the same, or shrinking? For example, if you provide programming to serve children's after-school needs in a community that projects significant growth of young families, replacing older persons who are leaving at retirement, your market (if you define it as the need for your programs) is growing, potentially quite dramatically. There are more opportunities but usually also more competitors in a growing market. On the other hand, if you are a provider of services to retired people in the same community, you are likely to see your market shrinking over the next few years.

TABLE 6.1. MARKET POSITION AND STRATEGY MATRIX.

Your Organization's Competitive Position	Number of Competitors in Market	Combined Market Trends (based on growing or shrinking customer base and growing or shrinking funding base)	Possible Strategies (Always ask if the strategy will advance your mission)	Is this a competitive or a collaborative strategy?
Strong	Many	Growing	Aggressively highlight your competitive advantages; address weaknesses that are competitive disadvantages; seek differentiation.	Competitive
		Shrinking	Consider acquisition of smaller direct competitors and indirect competitors, aiming for cost reduction.	Competitive
	Few	Growing	This is the optimal market situation. Continue what you are doing; look to strengthen your organization; continue innovating to maintain your edge; remain vigilant for new and up-and-coming competitors.	Competitive
		Shrinking	Continue what you are doing; address competitive disadvantages; consider acquisition of smaller direct competitors and indirect competitors to reduce cost.	Competitive
Middle: some strong competitive advantages, some competitive disadvantages	Many	Growing	Consider acquiring or partnering with direct competitors that can help address your competitive disadvantages and increase your share of this growing market. Seek differentiation from the pack.	Competitive or collaborative
		Shrinking	Consider acquiring or partnering with smaller direct competitors that can increase your market share and indirect competitors that can help you expand into new but related markets.	Competitive or collaborative

(Continued)

TABLE 6.1. MARKET POSITION AND STRATEGY MATRIX (CONTINUED).

Your Organization's Competitive Position	Number of Competitors in Market	Combined Market Trends (based on growing or shrinking customer base and growing or shrinking funding base)	Possible Strategies (Always ask if the strategy will advance your mission)	Is this a competitive or a collaborative strategy??
	Few	Growing	This is a good market situation. Address your competitive disadvantages; strengthen your organization and enhance its differentiation. Remain vigilant for new and up-and-coming competitors.	Competitive
		Shrinking	Strengthen your competitive position; address your disadvantages. Consider acquiring or partnering with smaller direct competitors to reduce cost.	Competitive or collaborative
Weak	Many	Growing	Strengthen your organization; address your competitive disadvantages. Consider partnering or merging with a larger, stronger organization. Focus on differentiating your organization from the pack.	Competitive or collaborative
		Shrinking	Either strengthen your organization (and seek a niche in this market) or consider exiting the market.	Competitive or exit strategy
	Few	Growing	Strengthen your organization; address your competitive disadvantages. Invest for long-term growth but beware of the likely entrance of new competitors if market growth continues.	Competitive
		Shrinking	Consider exiting this market, unless you are essential to customers.	Exit strategy

Another key factor affecting market trends is the availability of financial support for the type of programs you provide. For example, in a community hard hit by an economic downturn, third-party payers may decide to shift the weighting of their funding from arts programs to human services in order to meet a growing need for homeless services, economic development programs, and violence prevention. A symphony orchestra in this community will likely face a decline both in ticket sales and in third-party funding of all kinds. The symphony's market is shrinking, at least in the short term. The need it serves presumably remains the same: people still love symphonic music, although currently they are less able to afford to purchase tickets, so demand drops. Whether the symphony survives in the long term will partly depend on the competitive strategies it adopts (as discussed in Part Three) and partly on how soon the economy picks up again. Beyond size of the market, remember that market trends also include innovations in practice, changing demographics, and other big-picture issues that can impinge on your world.

Competition (Number of Competitors). Looking at your summary of market position (Worksheet 6.3), how competitive is the market you compete in? Are there many competitors or just a few? Few competitors may be a blessing, or there may be a message in the lack of competitors; is there a reason why no one else is in this market?

On each of these measures, there are many points between the yes-no choices I describe. There may be somewhere between "many" and "a few" competitors. While this factor could be represented on a continuum, for clarity's sake, in the Market Position and Strategy Matrix, I use a discrete variable: many/few. For simplicity, I have stuck to clear distinctions, but you need not. Use your judgment as to what works best for your situation.

Market Position (Competitive Position). You should now have a good overall sense of your position in the market. Looking at the ranking you gave your organization in relation to your competitors, ask your market research team to summarize your position: Are you a strong competitor (on balance you have many competitive advantages), a weak competitor (you have many competitive disadvantages), or do you fall somewhere in the middle (strong in some aspects, weak in others)?

Strong Position. As you can see, when your organization is a strong competitor, competitive approaches are generally the strategy of choice. You want to leverage your strength. If your organization is strong but not the market leader, your choice of strategies depends in part on market trends. If there are few competitors and the market is growing, competitive strategies may be optimal. In a shrinking market with many competitors, you may consider acquiring smaller players to consolidate the market. A new option also arises: exit from the market entirely. A strong competitor may wish to leave a shrinking market that it decides will not sustain it in the long run. By doing so, it leaves the market while still financially healthy, and it has time to plan for entry into a new market as well as for a graceful and responsible exit from the current, shrinking market. If you decide you cannot leave a shrinking market, perhaps for ethical reasons because you are the service provider of last resort, you may consider collaborative strategies such as partnerships with other organizations to reduce costs. You may also consider partnering or affiliating with indirect competitors who have strengths that complement yours and that may be in markets where the trends are more favorable.

Weak Position. If your organization is generally weak, aggressive competition may be out of the question, and collaborative strategies may be more effective. If you wish to choose a collaborative strategy, you may look to partner with a stronger organization or even to be acquired by one. If there are few competitors and the market is growing, however, competitive strategies may still be possible; consider strengthening your organization by aggressively addressing your competitive disadvantages. Then compete from a position of greater strength. Finally, if your organization is weak, there are many competitors, and the market is shrinking, a plausible option may be to exit.

Mixed Position. Of course, organizational life is seldom as simple as this configuration might suggest. Typically, a nonprofit might be one of several strong organizations in a changing market, delivering a service that has great value but is little recognized by society (for example, legal aid to the poor or arts education in urban schools). It might operate some programs that are top-notch and others that are in trouble, besieged by quality, effectiveness, or consistency concerns. If yours is such an organization, the Market Position and Strategy Matrix may help you to begin thinking about your competitive position. It might explain why you have not had as much success as you would like and perhaps also suggest some steps that might improve your position.

As I discussed in Chapter Three, there is a continuum of possible strategies, ranging from incidental/occasional, to medium intensity, to high intensity. At each level of intensity, you will need to make a decision regarding whether a competitive or a collaborative strategy is best. The fourth column of Table 6.1 provides an indication of which may be the strategy of choice.

Competitive Strategy Is a Process

Assessing where your organization might fall on the dimensions shown in Table 6.1 will require review and discussion of the brainstorming and analyses conducted earlier in this process. Choices will have to be made in interpreting these findings. The Market Position and Strategy Matrix is designed to help your organization think about the big picture. It is not a tool for decision making at the program level; those decisions can be made later, within the context of an organization-wide understanding of your market position.

Your market research team should work together to see which combination of factors seems to best describe your organization today. This process will shed light on organizational and market dynamics, helping you to better understand your position in the marketplace.

How you categorize your organization and market is somewhat subjective. By doing this as a group—with your market research team, board, senior management, and other key thinkers in your organization—you will be able to arrive at a more objective, sounder analysis. Remember that this is more of an art than a science. As you become increasingly familiar with your market, your competitors, and the trends in your market, and more knowledgeable about your organization's competitive advantages and disadvantages in this market, you will be able to refine your assessment. The market is constantly evolving. Hopefully, your actions in carrying out competitive strategies will help to change it in your favor. Regardless, you will need to monitor the market on an ongoing basis, and adjust your assessment as needed.

Strategy making involves piecing together a puzzle for which you have neither a template nor all the pieces. What's more, the pieces you do have and even the picture the finished puzzle is supposed to form are constantly evolving. The Market Position and Strategy Matrix portrays dimensions of market position, providing some puzzle pieces for your consideration in forming your organization's competitive strategy.

Competitive strategy is a process. There is seldom one right answer that is good for all eternity; what is important is the ongoing struggle with hard and soft data; keeping an open, objective mind; the development of sound instincts; and the constant testing of new ideas. An overreliance on analysis and overconfidence in hard data, according to Mintzberg, "can seriously bias and so distort any strategy making process" (1994, p. 258).

Strategy consists of decisions that must be made and implemented; actions that must be taken, monitored and evaluated; revisions to strategies; and implementation yet again. The process is ongoing. No exercise conducted at a single point in time can take the place of struggling with these issues on a regular basis.

That ongoing struggle is the essence of a successful strategy formation process and, ultimately, of successful competition.

Conclusion

This chapter has helped you to piece together the various elements of your market research to tell a story about where you stand today. Now that you have a good sense of your market position, you can consider strategies to strengthen it. This is the work of Part Three, which focuses on developing competitive strategies for your organization.

PART THREE

DEVELOPING COMPETITIVE STRATEGIES

The goals of this introduction are to orient you to the structure of each of the chapters in Part Three and then to provide you with a framework for thinking about competitive strategies. Given the range of situations in which competition is an effective strategic choice, you have most likely already identified circumstances in which it would be helpful to your organization to be more competitive. In addition, you were undoubtedly already using some competitive strategies before you opened this book, although you may not have thought of them in quite this way before. Remember to use your market research team to work through this section. The team's growing knowledge and confidence in the subject matter will be invaluable in piecing together the parts of your organization's story and developing your competitive strategies.

In Part Three, I present options for using ethical competitive strategies to address the market challenges you face. Specifically, I focus on strategies to secure four resources that are essential to your organization's success. Each of these is the topic of a separate chapter.

Chapter Seven suggests strategies for competing for customers.

Chapter Eight focuses on competing for third-party payers.

Chapter Nine offers competitive strategies to attract and retain executives, management, staff, board members, and other volunteers: your human resources.

Chapter Ten presents competitive strategies for cultivating the media to raise public awareness and support of your organization.

Each of the chapters has a similar format. Each begins with a brief description of the particular resource and its importance to your organization. Then, I discuss how to better understand your nonprofit's value to the holder of the resource. Each of these resource holders is a stakeholder in your organization. Essentially, your relationship to these resource holders is one of value exchange—a fundamental market function.

In Part Two, I stressed the importance of doing market research in order to learn from your customers. In Part Three, I suggest ways to use similar processes to learn about those who hold (that is, control) the resources you need. You must learn who they are and what they need from you.

Next, I discuss your strategic objectives for the particular resource under consideration. Do you need more or different customers, a wider array of third-party payers, or a more high-profile board? Determining your objectives involves examining the competitive advantages and disadvantages you have that are specific to the resource, using information you have already uncovered. You will consider your current market position and which competitors are strongest in that resource area. For example, if your reputation with the media is not as good as you would like, consider those organizations with great reputations. What does your research tell you about these competitors? What contributes to their competitive advantages? I will pose questions to help you better understand the underlying issues that may contribute to your competitive disadvantages.

Finally, I will suggest various strategies to strengthen your competitiveness in the particular resource area, based on where you stand in the market and where you want to be. Although you may be able to implement some of these necessarily generic strategies as presented, the process of considering them should also help you to create strategies tailored to your own circumstances. Each chapter ends with a brief reminder to assess your strategies on an ongoing basis to determine how well you are meeting your objectives and what adjustments you need to make.

The focus of Part Three is unabashedly on competitive strategies. As I have mentioned before, unlike collaborative strategies, these have not been adequately addressed in the nonprofit literature. This focus is not intended to diminish the role and value of collaboration in the nonprofit sector but rather to balance the excellent work that has been done on collaboration with an exclusive focus on competitive strategies.

What Does It Mean to Adopt a Competitive Strategy?

Before plunging into competitive strategies for specific situations and resource needs, I want to provide an overview of different approaches to competitive strategy. There are three general frameworks for competitive strategy. Depending on factors such as your market position, your resource needs, and your organization's culture or mind-set regarding competition, you may adopt one of the following approaches:

- Develop a *strategy of limited scope* to compete for a specific resource—for example, a new grant opportunity on the horizon.
- Apply *competitive strategic thinking*, wherein you inform your strategic thinking with an awareness of competitive issues but you do not overtly act competitively.
- Adopt an *organizational strategy of competitiveness* in which you decide to become overtly competitive, either in response to an external threat or as a strategy to attract resources.

Competitive Strategy as a Strategy of Limited Scope

In your daily work, you continually and perhaps often unconsciously adopt, implement, and revise strategies to achieve many ends. The decision to work with another nonprofit on anything from a joint grant proposal to a merger reflects a belief that the best means to an end in the situation is collaborative. This decision is easily understood because, as we have seen, it is consistent with the nonprofit sector's view of itself as inherently collaborative. Similarly, you may determine that the best means to a particular end is competitive. In fact, it is often possible for a given challenge to be successfully addressed either way. The choice does not require a decision to adopt an overall competitive or collaborative strategy. The decision is situational; it does not necessarily bring a larger meaning for your organization's strategic direction. Approached this way, competitive strategy is a strategy of limited scope.

Competitive Strategic Thinking

If you are unconcerned about the competitiveness of your environment, you may make decisions on how to move your agenda forward without considering how you fit into the larger market of your field of endeavor. You plan to accomplish X so you need Y resources. Your strategies are more programmatic than organizational in nature. However, if you see your environment as competitive, you will plan with an eye to what others in your market are doing to advance *their* agendas. Furthermore, your plans to attract resources will be made knowing that your competitors also desire those same resources. This is simply awareness of the market. No specific external threat or pressing competitive issue need be present. The nonprofit that considers its competitors' plans and impact on the market is simply making competition a consideration in strategic decision making.

An Organizational Strategy of Competitiveness

An organizational strategy of competitiveness is concerned with a nonprofit's overall approach to the market. Strategies tailored to specific situations may not be adequate to address a greater competitive threat, such as the potential entry into the market of a large new player or a technical innovation that threatens to render your work obsolete. In such situations, you may need to consider bold steps, alliances with other organizations, a big investment in marketing, or improved customer service. The competitive situation you face becomes the determining factor in your decision making.

The impetus to adopt an organizational strategy of competitiveness arises from a consideration of your overall position. It is usually a response to a sharpening of the competitive environment. Episodic competitive struggles for grants, board members, and media coverage may eventually become part of a greater, long-term struggle to attract resources. All the usual processes you use to assess the environment, determine strategy, and implement that strategy can be focused toward gaining needed resources. This is the most aggressive of the three competitive strategy frameworks I have presented.

If you choose to adopt an organizational strategy of competitiveness, you should recognize that this move carries risks as well as potential rewards. This is an aggressive stance, but one you should not be shy about adopting. Ask the following questions before undertaking an organizational strategy of competitiveness.

- Do we need substantial additional resources (for example, more customers, more staff, new board members or volunteers, more money, increased media attention) in order to advance our mission?
- Do we have a plan for using these additional resources (for example, serving additional customers) for mission advancement?

- Does the quality, effectiveness, and quantity of our work (and that of our competitors) justify us in attracting resources away from other nonprofits? That is, are we demonstrably more effective and efficient? Could we make better use of those resources than our competitors?
- Can we maintain or enhance a positive relationship with our customers, third-party payers, and other key stakeholders while becoming more competitive?
- Are we willing and able to manage any negative reaction to our increasingly overt competitiveness that may arise from other nonprofits in our field or community?

If you can honestly answer yes to each of these questions, then adopting an organizational strategy of competitiveness may be the right choice. However, you will run greater risks in adopting this approach than with either of the other two, because it flies in the face of our nonprofit cultural value of collaboration. Almost everyone would acknowledge the legitimacy of limited scope competition, without which the sector could not function. And a nonprofit that tries to inform its strategy with a competitive perspective may not appear more overtly competitive to outsiders. But a nonprofit that adopts competitiveness as an organizational strategy is likely to raise a stir. If your organization demonstrates ethical competition and effectiveness in meeting its customers' needs, this will work to counter the potential negatives.

Three Approaches, One Goal

What distinguishes competing for a specific resource using a limited-scope strategy from bringing an awareness of the competitive dimension to all strategic decision making or deciding to become more competitive overall as a key organizational strategy? The difference is in your end desire: Where are you going, and which type of strategy will get you there? The choice of approach is based on your resource needs; on an assessment of the external environment, including competitive threats and opportunities; and on a clear decision that this is the best strategy for your community or constituency at this time. The choice of a framework is not permanent or absolute. Successful nonprofits continually adjust in response to and in anticipation of environmental threats, constantly evolving in pursuit of their agenda. They also collaborate and compete in limited ways while pursuing overarching competitive strategies. Table III.1 portrays the key attributes of the three approaches to competitive strategy.

TABLE III.1. APPROACHES TO COMPETITIVE STRATEGY.

Competitive Strategies	Strategy of Limited Scope	Competitive Strategic Thinking	Organizational Strategy of Competitiveness
Character of approach	Focus only on resource that organization is currently contending for	Become highly aware of competitive issues in all decision making	Focus on becoming aggressively competitive as a core strategy to achieve desired position
Intent	To win the resource currently available	To ensure that strategic decisions are made with full awareness of competitive issues	To gain not only specific resources but the branding benefits of being a winner; to become a leader in the community or field
Possible behaviors	Write proposals, recruit board members, hire staff, solicit donors	Analyze competitive moves by other nonprofits and businesses in the market	Attempt to acquire or merge with weaker organizations; begin marketing campaign to position the nonprofit as a leader; invest in innovation
Anticipated reaction in the nonprofit sector	None; this is normal nonprofit behavior.	None; differences are not observable from the outside.	Potentially negative; others may see the nonprofit as too overtly competitive, not collaborative, although some will admire the nonprofit for this.

Conclusion

We have seen that there are three different approaches to competitive strategy and that these must flow from your intent—the objectives you have decided to accomplish in order to advance your mission. Keep the three approaches in mind as you read through the following chapters, each of which focuses on competing for a specific resource: customers, third-party payers, human resources of all kinds, or media and public attention.

CHAPTER SEVEN

CUSTOMERS

The goal of this chapter is to enhance your ability to compete for customers by developing specific strategies for gaining or keeping them. Even if your organization does not seek to serve ever more customers and does not compete with others for customers (perhaps there are more people in need of your programming than all competitors together can possibly serve), you probably want to keep the customers you have and replace those lost through normal attrition or program completion.

In a very real sense, all of your strategies are related to your customers—whether they are programmatic strategies aimed at directly meeting their needs so they experience positive outcomes from interacting with your organization, or competitive strategies intended to help you gain the resources to meet customer needs. This chapter focuses specifically on customers themselves as the resource for which you compete. It addresses the following question: How can you identify, attract, and keep customers, whether you want to increase your market share or just hold your own?

A Note on Organizational Size: Is Bigger Better?

When I discuss competitive strategies related to attracting and keeping customers, I am well aware that not all nonprofit organizations want to become bigger. However, many nonprofits do indeed want to grow, for a variety of reasons. A key motivator of growth comes from the fact that as a nonprofit reaches more people—if it maintains or enhances its effectiveness—it advances its mission that much more powerfully. When more people view your museum's collection, more members join your advocacy movement, or more children attend your school, the quality and impact of those experiences is shared by a larger group.

It is also true that larger organizations often are able to be more effective because they can afford to hire more and better trained staff, develop more sophisticated management processes, and keep abreast of developments in their field. As a result, they are able to secure a more stable supply of resources and they are better able to attract the attention of additional third-party payers, first-rate board members, and influential media. To be honest, another motivator of growth is the entrepreneurial spirit and innate competitiveness of many nonprofit leaders, who measure their own success, at least in part, by how successfully they grow their organizations. For many nonprofit executives, growth is what they like to do. While I don't mean to imply that bigger is necessarily better, I do want to acknowledge that bigger quite often means stronger.

Who Are Your Customers?

Most immediately, your customers are the people who participate in or benefit from your programs. In addition, the family members of those you directly interact with often can be thought of as customers. For example, if your programs serve children or youth, you may also in some ways serve these customers' parents, grandparents, or guardians. Similarly, if you provide programming for elderly adults, you may also consider these customers' adult children to be customers. In both cases, these "sandwiched" individuals secure your services on behalf of either their children or their elderly parents, but what makes them customers rather than third-party payers is that they usually join to some degree in their family member's participation in the program. At the very least, they are far more closely interested in the programmatic experience of a particular direct customer than a donor, government official, or foundation program officer.

Aside from the family members of directly served customers in these human services examples, a single nonprofit can have several different customer groups. For example, a symphony's customers may include ticket buyers who patronize its concerts, people who shop at its on-line store or eat in its on-site café, school districts that sponsor its music education activities in the classroom, and children who participate in these programs. An environmental advocacy organization may have members, who are customers because they are its primary constituents, but it may also develop scientific reports or briefings that it sells or distributes to policymakers, who are also then its customers.

To begin, think about your own organization's circumstances and make a list of all the types of customers, both direct and indirect, that your organization either currently serves or would like to attract. Remember, in my definition, a nonprofit's customers are the users of its programs, or the constituents of its cause. They are customers regardless of whether they directly pay anything at all for the benefits they receive.

It may seem a silly question to ask why your customers are important: after all, they have needs that your organization exists to meet. Keep in mind that the nonprofit economic model, particularly the unique intermediary role of third-party payers, can create a false sense of separation from your customers. If your organization is to compete effectively for customers, it is crucial that you not allow this separation between organization and customers to happen. The ongoing customer research I suggest in Part Two can go a long way toward keeping you in touch. Identifying the different types of customers you either serve or would like to serve, then articulating their different needs, is another way to keep in touch.

Understanding Your Customers' Needs

What do all these different customers you have identified need and potentially want from your organization? The findings from your market research will be useful in understanding some of the specific needs your customers have—what they want and need from your nonprofit or more generally from your field. For example, a member of the Sierra Club may ask, "What do I want to get from my participation in the environmental movement?" But there are also some needs that are nearly universal; most customer groups will share them, regardless of core business or field. These widespread needs include the following:

Individualization. Most of us want to be treated as individuals rather than as members of a group. Whether the grouping is environmentalists, adolescents, or drug addicts, most people want to be seen for who they are in their entirety and not labeled and responded to generically. Organizations that are highly effective in winning customer loyalty tend to have developed and to persistently work toward highly individualized responses to customers. While many of your customers' needs may in fact be identical, and so your programmatic responses to these needs may be highly developed and structured, even routine, no one wants to be treated like cattle passing through your organization's stile. To the customer, the program must feel like it is individually tailored.

Information. Another common customer need is for easy access to information. At a minimum, most people want to know what you do; where you are located; how to contact you; which staff members they will interact with; what, if anything, your program will cost them; and how it will benefit them. Some customers and other stakeholders—for example, potential board members—will want to know more. These people will ask what evidence you have of successful outcomes, how long you have been in business, how financially healthy you are, and whether you are well managed. You may have all of this information, and much more, readily available, at least in your head. But it does not meet your customers' and potential customers' need for information unless they can access it easily. Customer-friendly organizations have easily navigable Web sites and knowledgeable, friendly people who answer the phone and greet visitors.

Relationship. One last common customer need is for a relationship. Successful theater companies invite special patrons to backstage events at which they can meet the playwright. Customer-friendly human service agencies assign each client a single case manager who oversees and coordinates all aspects of their relationship with the organization. Fortune 500 companies sponsor regular Web chats and conference calls in which thousands of shareholders can be on-line—or on the line—with their CEO. The common thread here is that these are all attempts to give customers a sense of a personal relationship with a person, often with the leader of the organization. If you do not make an attempt to offer some form of relationship to your customers, your competitors will.

Your Organization's Objectives: What Do You Want to Achieve?

After completing Chapter Six, you should be well aware of the variety of strategies available to you, based on the combinations of market position and market dynamics in your organization's particular situation. You should also know who your competitors are, how many major competitors you have, whether they are direct or substitutable, and what their competitive advantages and disadvantages are in relation to your organization.

Now it's time to develop your competitive strategies. Start with your objectives. What market position do you have now, and what position would you like to have? Basically, there are three primary market objectives in regard to customers:

- You can seek to improve your market position by expanding your market share. This is the likely choice when you are not the top competitor but could still be a choice even if you are.

- You can try to maintain your market position and market share. This is a choice either when you are the top competitor or when the competitive challenges you face are so intense that you must work hard just to maintain your current position and market share.
- The last option is to shift, diversify, or remove your organization from the market. As I discussed in Chapter Six, this is a viable choice when your organization is a weak competitor and faces a tough uphill battle to change this situation—for example, if your programs are weak or the market is shrinking and there are many competitors.

The decision on which of these objectives to pursue should be informed by the three basic questions I listed in the introduction to Part One, the questions to ask as you develop competitive strategies:

- Where should we build on our strengths with further investment?
- Where should we redesign and improve our execution in order to raise quality?
- Where should we divest, transfer, or close in order to minimize loss or harm done?

The potential customer-focused objectives are as follows:

Improve your market position by expanding your market share. This is usually a choice intended to strengthen your market position. However, if your overall market is growing, this might also be an objective intended to maintain your position; that is, in an environment where all competitors are taking advantage of growth in the market, you may need to grow simply to maintain your current relative position. You may decide to pursue this objective for a variety of reasons, including threats to your current position. New threats may be due to new competitors entering your market or existing competitors pursuing their own objectives to expand their share of the market at your expense. You may also pursue this objective due to the inadequacy of other organizations serving the market, a situation that offers an opening to make your programs more widely available. If the market is truly inadequately served, you may also feel compelled by your mission to step in and address unmet needs.

Maintain your market position and market share. This is most often an objective to simply maintain your current position by keeping your customer base. However, it could also be chosen when you want to improve your position. For example, the market may be shrinking, and as a result, other competitors may decide or be forced to leave the market. By deciding to stay in the market, maintaining your customer base, you may actually improve your market position in relation to the remaining competitors.

You might pursue such an objective due to a decision that you are at the optimal size. Bigger does not always mean better. For example, you may decide that rather than pouring your energy into growth during a difficult economic period, you will focus instead on addressing your competitive disadvantages, particularly any programmatic or administrative weaknesses, in order to be ready to expand should you choose to do so—or if the opportunity presents itself—in the future.

This objective might be pursued in combination with the third objective by expanding into other customer markets. That is, you may decide to maintain your current customer base but also to expand by providing new programming that is complementary. An example of this might be a homeless shelter and a soup kitchen that decide to combine forces in order to better serve their shared customer base. This objective may entail either collaborative strategies if pursued in partnership with another organization, as in this example, or competitive strategies if you decide to acquire or build the new program on your own. Of course, the strategy of pursuing complementary programming should be undertaken only if there is a good alignment between the current and proposed activities and if the strategy helps you to better advance your mission.

Shift, diversify, or remove your organization from the market. You might choose this objective if your market research reveals that the customers you serve (your actual customers) are largely not your targeted or intended customers or are not those who could most benefit from your programs, or if a new market seems a more promising route to mission fulfillment. This is an objective undertaken, often with great difficulty, to improve your effectiveness in advancing your mission. In this case, your strategy may be to alter your approach to obtaining customers (for example, through changed communications or marketing tactics) or to alter your programs to attract your desired customers. Circumstances that might lead you to choose this objective are more common than you might think.

I encountered a particularly harrowing example of this situation when I was an executive director. My organization entered into merger negotiations with a nonprofit preschool whose mission was to serve emotionally disturbed three-to-five-year-olds. This was a good complementary fit with our services, which were focused on emotionally disturbed five-to-twelve-year-olds. In the course of our due diligence process, however, we discovered that over time the preschool had developed an expertise in serving not emotionally disturbed children, its stated target market, but preschoolers with communication handicaps. In California, services for these two groups of children are funded through entirely separate governmental channels. The preschool was deeply devoted to its actual little customers and did a fine job with them, but when its prime funder, the county mental health department, discovered whom it was serving, it promptly called for a program audit, disallowed the entire program, and demanded reimbursement for several years worth of funding. Ultimately, the merger went forward, and we avoided repayment of nearly a million dollars in disallowed costs on the condition that we close the program. We ended up owning the preschool's building, but with no program. It took us several years to restart a therapeutic nursery school with the appropriate funding *and* customer base.

You might also decide to diversify your customer base by focusing program efforts on different customer market segments. For example, if you are working for an environmental advocacy organization working to clean up toxic sites and your members tend to be middle- and upper-income suburban supporters, you might decide to try to bring in urban and lower-income members, who live where many of the toxic sites are located. This does not reflect a change in mission but rather a broadening of the constituency you hope to engage in your work.

Your market research team has enough information in hand to determine, at this point, a set of objectives about your customers. This choice can always be modified as circumstances change, but for now, what is it? Try to write it in a sentence. Here are some examples:

- We need to double the number of our customers in the eighteen-to-twenty-two-year-old group in order to become more of a force with third-party payers and receive public recognition for being a leader in our field.
- We plan to keep our current customer base of about three thousand, even while others are leaving the market. If we can hang on, we will become the market leader, and that position will help us to attract the resources we need, even in this lousy economy.
- We are going to stop our failing efforts to recruit boys to our music program and instead focus on our core strength, the 80 percent of our customers who are girls. We can be the best girls' program in the country.

Selecting, Developing, and Implementing Your Strategies

Next, I will describe a process for selecting, developing, and implementing your strategies for achieving your objectives.

Strategies for Expanding Your Customer Base

As described earlier, this objective is usually reasonable in a growing market. It is particularly useful when there are many players in the market and you need to do one of the following:

- Increase your market share in order to better advance your mission by serving more people

- Strengthen your organizational capacity by increasing its revenues and therefore the amount you can spend on infrastructure investments such as computer systems, communications vehicles, and management staff
- Increase revenues to provide a financial cushion or to grow out of a difficult plateau size at which the organization has inadequate operating revenues to manage its complexity. (Uncomfortable plateaus often occur in nonprofits with annual operating budgets around $500,000, $3 million, and again at $10 million.)
- Differentiate your organization in the public's eye in order to attract a range of necessary resources

While working to concentrate resources in your organization and then using your greater size to attract still further resources at the expense of others in your market may seem unfair, it is the reality: the more resources you have, the more resources you can attract!

Compare your organization's competitive advantages and disadvantages in customer and program areas, and complete Worksheet 7.1, drawing on your earlier work. Include your major direct and substitutable competitors, as many as you identified in Worksheet 6.1, where the required information will be found. For areas in which you have competitive advantages, determine how you can either build on them or publicize them to potential customers. If you have competitive disadvantages in relation to your competition, seek out, study, and learn from organizations that have competitive advantages in those areas. Return to the exercises you completed in Chapter Six. Extract the analyses of organizational relatedness from the relevant copies of Worksheet 6.1, and transfer the scores on competitors' advantages and disadvantages in the areas of customers and programs from the last column of Worksheet 6.2. Enter the information in Worksheet 7.1. These advantages are most likely to fall into the following two categories:

- *Reputation.* Whether or not your competitors deserve their great reputation, the fact is that if they have a better reputation than your organization does, you need to learn why and then use this knowledge to improve yours.
- *Customer satisfaction.* This refers to the satisfaction of your past, current, and potential customers with their interactions with your organization and its people. There are various dimensions of satisfaction, including satisfaction with the following:
  Services, including whether your programs are effective and whether they are the right approach for the needs you address
  Access to services, which has a variety of dimensions, including location, financial issues, hours of operation, friendliness and receptivity of staff and volunteers, linguistic barriers, and cultural appropriateness

WORKSHEET 7.1. COMPARISON OF COMPETITORS' ADVANTAGES AND DISADVANTAGES IN COMPETING FOR CUSTOMERS.

Competitor's Name	Total Relatedness Score	Customer Relatedness Score	Service Relatedness Score	Geographic Relatedness Score	Competitive Score (Customers)	Competitive Score (Programs)

Play to Win by David La Piana, ISBN 0-7879-6813-7, cloth, copyright © 2005 Jossey-Bass, An Imprint of Wiley.

Quality, including program quality (do programs produce the intended out-comes?), program staff quality (do staff members have the right qualifica-tions, training, and attitudes?), and quality of the facilities where programs are delivered (are facilities safe, clean, and appealing?)

Ask yourself what you can learn from your competitors' strengths. What should you do to strengthen your organization? You may learn that your disadvantages are more perceived than real and thus the main areas you need to strengthen are your marketing and customer communications. You may, however, learn that your competitive disadvantages are tied to real issues, such as the following:

- *Access to your services,* including where you are located, the hours you operate, and the languages your staff and volunteers speak.
- *Affordability,* meaning the amount your customers must pay for services. Exam-ples include a co-payment for health services, the ticket price for an arts perfor-mance, or a membership fee to belong to your organization. Although the true cost of services in the nonprofit sector is typically subsidized to some degree, often the subsidized price still is out of reach for many potential customers.
- *Acceptability,* including cultural competence, the quality of your facilities, and the qualifications and personalities of your staff.

If your organization faces any of these issues, look to competitors who have competitive advantages in these areas and learn from them. Include in your analy-ses any organizations that are models in your field. Look outside your immediate geographic area to find these organizations. Draw on your peer network to iden-tify similar organizations all over the country. As I mentioned earlier, since these organizations probably are not your direct competitors, their staff members may be very willing to share with you their strategies for achieving competitive advantages.

Determine what changes you need to make to turn your "disadvantage" or "neutral" assessments into advantages, then secure any resources needed to implement this strategy.

Examine Worksheet 7.1 for direct and substitutable competitors who have advantages over your organization in their customer and program areas. Enter the names and market position of these competitors in the middle column of Worksheet 7.2. Then, using the information you have previously collected for these organizations, complete the "Comments" column.

When completed, Worksheet 7.2 provides a good idea of the areas of your organization you may need to strengthen in order to better serve both your cur-rent and potential customers. You may learn that your competitors' advantages

WORKSHEET 7.2. ORGANIZATIONS WITH COMPETITIVE ADVANTAGES IN CUSTOMER OR PROGRAM AREAS.

Area	Competitors with Advantages (include market position/rank)	Comments
Customers (overall)		
Satisfaction with services		
Market perception of organization/reputation		
Market share (large market share = advantage; small market share = disadvantage)		
Programs (overall)		
Quality of programs		
Effectiveness of programs		
Focus on mission		

are primarily related to perceptions. The market may perceive a particular competitor quite positively or in general may perceive your organization negatively. More likely, however, is nonperception: you simply may be unknown to the market compared to one or more competitors. Whatever the case may be, you need to change the market's perception of your organization.

The most useful strategy for addressing this objective is usually pursued through enhancing communications with your customers, highlighting your outcomes, and featuring satisfied customers in your materials and messages. Consider using any testimonials you captured in your customer research. You can also create case studies that document programmatic successes. Nothing tells your organization's story better than your satisfied customers.

You can communicate with potential customers through a variety of vehicles, ranging from traditional—and very expensive—purchased media advertising to an enhanced Web site (if that is an appropriate vehicle for reaching your intended customers) to free public service announcements on television and radio stations. Printing a newsletter or brochure is a popular communications approach among nonprofits, but before you invest in these expensive and static devices, carefully consider how you will deliver them to their intended readers. Leaving a stack of brochures out on a table in your waiting room is not the best approach to marketing if you want to gain new customers.

You may come to believe that there are few competitors with advantages over your organization when it comes to attracting customers. If your organization is clearly more effective than your competitors and customers seem to prefer it, you may seek to expand by competing for your competitors' customers. A key strategy to support this objective is more aggressive marketing—that is, more effective communication with your market. As you will hear again in the succeeding chapters, communication is an essential supportive strategy for securing any needed resource.

A question to ask yourself before embarking on a course to grow your customer base is whether you have both the organizational and programmatic capacity to serve more customers. Many nonprofit growth efforts falter because either program quality and responsiveness decreases as programming expands or administrative support for additional customers fails in such crucial areas as billing, record keeping, and data tracking. Another critical question is whether there is indeed more need *and demand* for your programming among your intended customers and in your defined geographic area than you and your market competitors currently are meeting. It is both easier and more politically palatable to compete for unserved customers than to attempt to attract a competitor's current customers away.

If you can answer both of these questions "yes," then your strategy may be to increase your marketing efforts so that more potential customers know about your organization and develop a positive perception of it. If you do not have the capacity to serve more customers, then you may seek to increase your capacity by acquiring or partnering with other competitors. This can be achieved by identifying competitors that are a good match for your organization, such as those serving contiguous areas with similar programs. Before you embark on this path, however, you must consider any competitive disadvantages of the organizations in question, as revealed in your earlier competitor analyses, and ensure that none are significant enough to become a detriment to your own organization should you associate with them. Ideally, you want to partner with organizations that have complementary competitive advantages, so that you strengthen one another. *The Nonprofit Mergers Workbook* can help with this assessment (La Piana, 2000).

You may also seek to expand your customer base by increasing your own programmatic capacity. This may be a reasonable strategy if there are no suitable organizations to acquire or partner with or if the market is growing and thus greater overall customer-serving capacity is needed; that is, if the existing organizations do not, taken together, have the programmatic capacity to meet the current or projected demand for a particular program.

Of course, increasing your programmatic capacity so that you can serve more customers involves securing other resources, particularly increased funding and additional human resources, as well as, quite possibly, additional facilities from which to offer the program. These considerations must be part of your decision to expand.

Specific strategies for expanding your customer base include these:

- Look for unserved customers in less-than-obvious places. If the market for traditional ballet goers is saturated, try taking your show to a new audience: invite immigrants, teens, or others who could enjoy the experience to visit the ballet and arrange for them to meet the dancers; they might become customers.
- Similarly, move your program activities to where the potential customers are. Schools, recreation centers, and the facilities of other, unrelated, nonprofits can be good places to meet new customers.
- If your research has shown that potential customers are most concerned about cost, hours, or other accessibility issues, redesign at least parts of your program to meet these needs.
- It may seem obvious, but advertise that you have openings for new clients or members. Unless you do, many potential customers may think you are full.
- Market: communicate, communicate, and then communicate some more, targeting your messages at intended customers and third-party payers who support them. Highlight any of the strategies described earlier; they are of no use if your intended audience does not hear about them.

Strategies for Maintaining Your Current Customer Base

In a dynamic marketplace, you can never rest on your laurels and simply assume that your customers will continue to use your services. Moreover, if, as in many organizations, your customer base continually turns over due to the nature of your work, you cannot just assume that you will continue to have a steady stream of new customers walking in the door. If you target customers of a particular age range (preschoolers); meet the needs of people in a particular stage of life transition (divorce); or if your programs are necessarily time-limited (season tickets), you have built-in customer turnover. Even lifelong programs such as YMCA memberships lose customers through attrition, especially in our highly mobile society.

While it is hard work for most nonprofits to continually replace or renew customers just to hold their ground in the market, there are some positive aspects of customer turnover. One benefit is the possibility of an ever-increasing pool of satisfied former customers who will spread positive messages about their experience with your program. (Think about university alumni programs.) Another benefit of customer turnover is that it enables outcome measurement. If customers have clear entrance and exit dates, this allows for easier preprogram and postprogram comparisons to measure program impact and assess your outcomes, which hopefully will yield success data that can be used for marketing purposes.

In order to develop strategies for maintaining your customer base, you need to conduct the same type of analysis of your competitive advantages and disadvantages that was described earlier for organizations that want to expand their customer base. (You can use Worksheets 7.1 and 7.2.) There is no easy way to know how much effort will produce a stable customer base versus one that is growing or declining, so you will need to constantly monitor both your customer numbers (including customer use of your programs) and your marketing efforts in order to keep them in line with your objectives. Some specific strategies for keeping your customer base stable include these:

- Monitor your competitors' efforts to ensure that they are not trying to lure your customers away. If they are, you need to know about it as soon as possible, so that you can develop counterstrategies.
- Develop long-term or repeat customer recognition programs such as special backstage passes or preferred seating, discounts for early or extended renewal of membership dues, and promotions that recognize long-term or repeat customers in your publicity.
- Fine-tune your customer feedback mechanisms. An organization that seeks stability cannot afford to alienate long-term customers.

Strategies for Shifting or Diversifying Your Customer Base

If your objective is to shift or diversify your customer base, you will need to conduct an analysis similar to the ones in the preceding two sections (again, using Worksheets 7.1 and 7.2), but in addition to analyzing direct and substitutable competitors, include any indirect competitors from Worksheet 6.4 that offer programs that are complementary to yours. Among your direct competitors, do any offer complementary services, making them also indirect competitors?

If you are seeking to diversify, you might consider acquisition of a competitor or of a competitor's program that is complementary to your own offerings. It may be that another organization would be willing to divest itself of a program that is tangential to its mission or even to exchange programs with you, as MacMillan (1983) suggests. If you also have a tangential program that would fit better in your colleague's organizational mix, exchanging could be a win-win proposition. Such transactions, while never easy, are accomplished in order to help both parties concentrate more fully on their core competencies and programs.

Some specific strategies for shifting or diversifying your customer base include these:

- Identify organizations with programs that are related to yours but do not directly compete. If your assessment shows that they are programmatically weak or ineffective, develop a marketing strategy to let their customers know about what you do. You need not say that your program is better; their customers are probably dissatisfied, and some will give you a try if they just know you exist.
- Find an unserved market segment that is in line with your mission (for example, your organization is a health care advocate, but no one currently provides advocacy at the state level for regulating the use of psychotropic and antidepressant medications with teens). Work with potential customers (family members, physicians, therapists) to raise public awareness of both the need that is currently unmet and your programmatic solution to the problem. By following this type of strategy, you can be first to market in a new or emerging area.
- Be aware of technological innovations that may offer opportunities as well as threats. For example, if cable programming is threatening to keep some of your theater's customers at home, consider developing your own cable programming. In doing so, you may reconnect with your traditional customers as well as identify a new market with new customers—people who never go to theaters but prefer to watch television.

What If Your Organization Is Not Effective?

I have based this discussion on the assumption that your organization is capable and effective; as I have emphasized, you should only undertake increased competitiveness if your nonprofit is clearly effective at what it does. If this is not the case, your objective should be, first and foremost, to improve your organization's capacity and performance. If the analysis you conducted in Chapter Six reveals that you are a weak competitor, your strategies must focus on turning your competitive disadvantages into advantages. Until then, you will be in a position to consider a limited-scope competitive strategy (in everyday activities such as submitting grant applications and recruiting board members) and competitive strategic thinking (infusing all your strategic thinking with an awareness of competitive issues in your market), but it will not be appropriate to launch an aggressive organizational strategy of competitiveness. This level of competitiveness requires, from both an ethical and a practical perspective, a sound performance base.

Assessing Your Outcomes

Prior to implementing a competitive strategy, make sure you have put in place a structure and process for measuring its impact. The customer research that I have suggested is a good starting point. Ultimately, you will need to identify what outcomes you expect to achieve from your strategy. If you seek to expand, identify by how much, in what timeframe, and at what expense. If your expansion will entail a capital or operating outlay during the planning and start-up, where will these funds come from? Consider the impact of growth on your existing customer base and the broader community. How can you minimize any negative impact while maximizing the positive?

Whatever your objective, identify how you will measure success, and be prepared to make changes early on if you find that you are not achieving your desired outcomes. Measures of success might include the number of additional customers served, the types of customers, and the impact of your programs on these customers. Identify how you will obtain this information, and make sure the processes are in place to facilitate its capture and analysis. With hard work over a long period of time, and a bit of luck, you will move closer to your desired market position, attracting and maintaining the types and numbers of customers you seek.

CHAPTER EIGHT

THIRD-PARTY PAYERS

The goal of this chapter is to help you develop strategies to secure the funding you need to supplement earned income from your customers. If you are that rare nonprofit that exists completely on customer payments, then you might want to skip this chapter. Here you will identify potential third-party payers, determine how well your work is aligned with their needs and interests, and assess how well you are meeting their expectations. You will consider how to strengthen your relationships with third-party payers and anticipate future trends. You will consider which third-party payers fund your competitors and how you might appeal to them as well. This process will be helpful no matter what objectives and market position you seek.

This chapter is not about fundraising. Many resources already exist on that topic. They teach a nonprofit how to cultivate, solicit, and steward donors of all kinds, and they are often quite practical. The focus here, rather, is on strategies for competing for financial resources. The difference is between seeking funds and competing for them—an awareness of who else seeks funds from the same third-party payers as you do and what you can do to win the race.

After assessing how to strengthen your funding base, you determine what implications your customer objectives and desired market position have for your funding needs—what strategies you need in regard to your third-party payers. If you plan for a more prominent market position and a larger customer base, for example, your organization may require expansion funding. If you are in a rapidly growing and increasingly competitive market, you may need additional funding to meet a growing need regardless of whether your strategy is to maintain or grow your current customer base. A niche strategy could involve exiting parts of your market to concentrate on areas where you have the greatest competitive advantage. This strategy might entail a shift away from some current third-party payers and toward new ones whose interests are aligned with your niche. In this chapter, I describe strategies to address these and other scenarios.

Who Are Your Third-Party Payers?

Third-party payers include units of government, private insurers, philanthropic foundations, corporate giving programs, and individual donors. Third-party payers are an essential element of the nonprofit economic model. They are not direct customers; they do not directly and personally benefit from the services they fund. They can, however, be considered indirect customers because they do receive something of value in return for their funding. Determining what that something is and how to highlight it to a particular third-party payer are the keys to success.

Cultivating and maintaining good relations with third-party payers is critical to a strong market position. Consider their reasons for supporting you. Some third-party payers, such as foundations, see themselves as investing in the nonprofits they support. They have an interest in your success and often want to monitor their investment. Others, such as insurers and government, are purchasing services and may profess no larger interest in you than that. For most nonprofit executives, attracting and keeping third-party payers is a major effort. It is important to understand the value they receive from your organization, while never forgetting that it does not exist to serve third-party payers but rather works with them to advance its mission. This formula works best when you align with funders that share a commitment to your mission.

This chapter shows how to learn the needs and interests of third-party payers. Begin by completing Worksheet 8.1 for the current and the past two years. Add any projected sources of third-party funding for the upcoming year. Consider which third-party payers will continue to fund your nonprofit next year. If you don't think one will continue, be sure to indicate why.

Now expand your list to potential third-party payers, drawing on your knowledge of who funds similar programs in your geographic area. Consider the competitor research you conducted earlier. Review your direct competitors. What are their sources of funding? Often this information is available on an organization's Web site. Look at your indirect competitors as well. Specifically, examine those who have particularly strong finances. In addition, consider

WORKSHEET 8.1. SOURCES OF FUNDING.

Type of Funder	Name	Purpose of Funding	Baseline Year (2 years before current year)		Last Year		Current Year		Next Year (projected)	
			Amount ($)	Percentage of Total Funding for Year	Amount ($)	Percentage of Total Funding for Year	Amount ($)	Percentage of Total Funding for Year	Amount ($)	Percentage of Total Funding for Year
Government										
Private insurers										
Philanthropic foundations										
Corporations										
Individual donors (major)*										
Earned income (payment from direct customers for services or products)	N/A	(services/products)								
	N/A	(services/products)								
	N/A	(services/products)								
Other										
Total Funding				100%		100%		100%		100%

*Define "major" in terms of your organization. What constitutes a particularly large gift? This might be $500, $1,000, $5,000, or more. List your top five to ten individual donors.

Play to Win by David La Piana, ISBN 0-7879-6813-7, cloth, copyright © 2005 Jossey-Bass, An Imprint of Wiley.

programs that are similar to yours but are located in other geographic areas; do they have national or regional sources of funding that might be interested in funding your programs? Incorporate information on all of these potential third-party payers in Worksheet 8.2.

Understanding the Needs of Third-Party Payers

While each third-party payer certainly has its own interests and needs, there are some common needs that all will likely share. The key components of success with third-party payers are positive relationships, performance, and accountability for funds received. Nonprofits that meet these needs have a significant competitive advantage over their competitors. Let's review each component in turn.

Relationships

Relationships are key. The ability to form and maintain a positive rapport with the person making the funding decision is essential. In the case of an individual donor, this is the donor himself or herself. With philanthropic foundations, it is the program officer who will make the grant recommendation to the president and board, to whom you may have no access. Government contracts are a little more complicated, since you may initially respond to a bid process but later have an opportunity to form a relationship with the staff person who will manage the contract, as well as, in the case of local government at least, with the elected officials who ultimately will approve the selection.

Always view the current gift, grant, or contract as an audition for the next one. Ongoing support should not be considered a guarantee, but neither is it limited to the level of the first commitment. An initial foundation grant of $20,000 may lead to a larger, multiyear commitment of several hundred thousand dollars. An initial contract to support one weekend of performances may lead to a deeper, long-term commitment to the development of a new production.

Because it is difficult to measure outcomes in many spheres of nonprofit activity and also because of the workload, skill set, and philosophy of third-party payers (for example, the common desire among foundation staff to avoid micro-management of grantees), they often do not have in-depth knowledge of the nonprofits they support. Thus, third-party payers of all kinds rely to some degree on their trust and faith in the leaders of the entities they fund. Devoting time to cultivating their trust is very worthwhile. Foundation officials are fond of saying, "We fund people, not organizations."

WORKSHEET 8.2. POTENTIAL SOURCES OF FUNDING.

Name of Potential Third-Party Payer	Type (for example, government, foundation, corporation, individual donor)	Types of Programs Funded in Recent Years	Competitors Who Are Funded by This Payer	Typical Range of Grant, Contract, or Gift ($)	Comments

Play to Win by David La Piana, ISBN 0-7879-6813-7, cloth, copyright © 2005 Jossey-Bass, An Imprint of Wiley.

Performance

Performance is the ability to deliver as promised in the exchange relationship—to accomplish what was promised in return for the funds. These days, third-party payers are increasingly concerned about the effectiveness of the organizations they support. To the extent that you can demonstrate the effectiveness of your programs or, at a minimum, that you at least recognize the importance of outcomes assessment and have a measurement program in place, you will stand out among organizations competing for many sources of funding.

Some third-party payers will place more emphasis than others on the fund seeker's ability to deliver actual results (for example, reduced teen pregnancy) as opposed to merely make efforts in the right direction (for example, providing one hundred teens with counseling). While the emphasis varies, almost all sources of funds want to know whether the services or activities were effective in addressing the identified challenge. What is most important is to be clear and consistent about how you measure the impact of your organization and to make sure that the measures you choose are realistic and aligned with your mission. They need not be complicated, expensive, or highly formal, but they must tell a convincing story. If you are clear about the basis of your assessment when you seek and obtain funds, you and your supporter will both have the same expectations. Your job is then, of course, to deliver on those expectations.

Accountability

Finally, you must be responsible for how your finances and other resources are managed, safeguarded, and expended. This is accountability. Accountability is different from the question of succeeding at addressing a problem. Especially these days, most third-party payers, including many individual donors, want assurances that their money has been used for the intended purpose (that is, the services were in fact provided or the activities completed), whether or not the intended outcomes were achieved. They want to know that the nonprofit at least tried to do what it promised to do. And they want to know that the organizations they fund uphold high ethical standards while making the effort.

Analyzing Your Third-Party Payers' Needs and Interests

Beyond relationships, performance, and accountability, what are the needs and interests of your third-party payers? To answer this question, start by examining the information you entered in Worksheet 8.1. What story does it tell? Where does most of your funding come from? Is your organization highly dependent on just one or a few third-party payers or on just one type of funder? For most organizations, lack of diversity in sources of funding, and the resulting dependence on just a few funders, is not healthy. In fact, it can put the organization at serious risk. Relying primarily on, for example, philanthropic foundations for funding is akin to both people in a couple working for the same company. In the short-term, it may be convenient, but a downturn in the economy that might have been difficult (fewer grant funds for the nonprofit, a lost job for the couple), becomes catastrophic. Aside from economic cycles, if a key third-party payer on which you depend decides to change its focus to another type of program or to another subsector altogether, you will be left in a very precarious situation.

An organization that is heavily dependent on government funding is especially at risk. As we all know, there are no long-term guarantees of government funding; a poor economy or a change in administrations can cause an immediate shift in priorities. I once worked with a nonprofit substance abuse counseling center that had received some years before a five-year federal grant to improve the quality of treatment by improving the salaries of its counselors. The grant was used as intended, to raise the staff's salaries and benefits substantially. With only a few months left on the last year of the grant, the center's executive director was panicking. "We can't cut salaries back to where they used to be," he moaned. "Everyone will quit." He was right. There was no way the new salaries could be sustained with the center's business model, and when the grant ended, many of the staff did indeed quit. In the end, the center actually closed down as a result of the end of this grant. This is not the only time that I have seen a nonprofit go out of business when a large, multiyear grant or contract ends.

As you review the information in Worksheet 8.1, examine the trends in your funding over time—from the baseline year to the current year. What does this indicate about the future? Have any third-party payers stopped funding your organization in the past few years? Do you know why? Do you know why your current third-party payers fund your organization? What has changed over time in the reasons why your organization gets funding? Complete Worksheet 8.3.

Talking with Your Funders

Your next step is to begin a conversation with your third-party payers and with the potential funders you listed in Worksheet 8.2. Just as you did with your direct customers, you need to survey these indirect customers. While it can be time-consuming, I highly recommend that you talk with your current and recent third-party payers in person or by phone. This one-on-one interaction establishes and strengthens your relationship with them. It gives you a chance to update them on your organization (or, in the case of potential supporters, to introduce

WORKSHEET 8.3. SUMMARY DESCRIPTION OF FUNDING AND CHANGES IN FUNDING IN RECENT YEARS.

	Our funding has . . . (check one)	Our third-party payers are . . . (check one)	Over the past few years, our third-party payers have . . . (check one)	The reasons why we obtain funding have . . . (check one)	Our relationships with our third-party payers are . . . (check one)
Level 1: Strong	_____ Increased	_____ Diversified	_____ Become more diversified; increased in number	_____ Remained the same	_____ Positive overall
Level 2: Mixed	_____ Remained the same	_____ Somewhat diversified	_____ Remained steady	_____ Changed somewhat	_____ Neutral overall
Level 3: Weak	_____ Decreased	_____ Focused on one or two primary funders	_____ Declined in number	_____ Changed a lot	_____ Nonexistent (do not have relationships) or negative
Comments	Comments, specific third-party payers	Comments, specific third-party payers	Comments, specific third-party payers	Comments, specific third-party payers	Comments, specific third-party payers

Play to Win by David La Piana, ISBN 0-7879-6813-7, cloth, copyright © 2005 Jossey-Bass, An Imprint of Wiley.

them to it) and gives them a chance to ask you questions. Similarly, when you ask questions (for example, about their interests), a live discussion allows you to ask follow-up questions to ensure that you have understood their responses. Your attempts at securing an initial meeting and subsequent relationship building with representatives from foundations, corporations, and government agencies, and even with potential major individual donors, will be more fruitful if you follow these guidelines:

- If possible, start by interviewing people you already know, however slightly; perhaps you could choose a program officer at a foundation with which you have a current grant.
- When requesting a meeting, tell the person up front that you are not coming to ask for money. Third-party payers are besieged by requests for meetings in which nonprofit leaders want to pitch their organization. Let the person know that you are actually more interested in their ideas than their money. Frame some topics to give them a taste of what the meeting will be like. You might say something like, "I want to ask you where you think this field is going over the next ten years." Avoid saying, "I want to ask you about what your foundation funds." This information is available in their materials and is a clear sign, for the person whom you want to interview, that a pitch meeting is being proposed.
- Focus the meeting on substantive topics, as advertised, not on touting the achievements of your organization. Discuss the current issues of the larger field you are in, and then place your organization in this larger context. While you would love to know what this person thinks of your organization, it is probably not going to be possible to ask outright, at least not yet.
- Be yourself. If the person has a picture of a kids' soccer team on his desk, ask if he coaches. Making a personal connection is important, but you must be sensitive to the boundaries people are comfortable with. We have all had initial meetings with people who actually prefer to spend the first half hour talking about their and your family before getting down to business, but others would find this intrusive.
- Honor your time allotment. If you asked for thirty minutes, stick to it, unless you are invited to continue longer. Toward the end of your time, ask about additional people the person thinks you should talk to. Use the person's name, with his or her permission, to get a meeting with others whom you do not know.
- You have told the person this is not going to be a pitch meeting; stick to this commitment! The only exception to this rule is if the person shows great interest in your organization and then asks "So, how can I help?" Even in this situation, say that you really do not want to turn this into a grantseeking meeting,

that you sincerely just want to ask her or his opinion but that you would be happy to describe a few of your current projects or priorities. Then, after the meeting, follow up.

- Now that you have established a relationship, keep it going. Send the person the occasional professional article that you think he might be interested in, with your card clipped to it. Call and ask her opinion on a new development in the field, or invite him to your next open house. Avoid being a pest, but try to build a relationship. The key is to do whatever you do with sincerity.

Using this process, prepare and conduct interviews with as many past, current, and potential third-party payers as possible, using the lists in Worksheets 8.1 and 8.2. Some will refuse to meet or speak with you at all, and others will do so once but not respond to further overtures, but a few may begin to reciprocate your attempts at reaching out to them.

Before you call to set up an interview, do some research to learn about the third-party payer's current funding priorities. For organizations (foundations, corporations, government), you can usually find this information by visiting their Web site. The level of research you need to do will vary, depending on how close a relationship you have with the subject. Consider the summary information you entered in Worksheet 8.3. If you do not have a close relationship with your third-party payers, now is the time to begin. As I have said, funding in our sector is similar to any other market exchange; it is built on relationships of trust.

Your Organization's Objectives: What Do You Want to Achieve?

As in all things, knowing what you want to accomplish relative to your organization's third-party payers is crucial to getting there. But first it is important to know where you are currently positioned.

Current Position: Can You Get There from Here?

In Chapter Seven, you determined your desired market position with customers, then developed strategies to achieve it. Now consider the funding you need to make this a reality. Regardless of the position you seek, one of your organizational mandates is to be financially stable. Prior to implementing strategies to help you achieve the market position you want, it is important to determine whether you have the financial resources to implement your programmatic strategies. Shifts in programming, new initiatives, and program development efforts can all cost money. While some dedicated funding may be available through grants and donors interested in strengthening your organization, you may need to use reserves to supplement these new funding sources.

Be sure to budget carefully. One common mistake in both the business and the nonprofit worlds is developing projections that are too optimistic in the early going of a new venture. Start-up costs may be significantly higher than expected, and hoped for revenues from new programs or a larger market share may be slow to materialize. It is best to plan conservatively.

Desired Position: Securing the Funds to Get There

In Chapter Seven, I discussed the three primary choices in regard to your organization's market position. You can choose to

- Improve your market position by expanding your market share
- Maintain your market position and market share
- Shift, diversify, or remove your organization from the market

Your ability to be successful in securing and maintaining any of these positions is tied to your financial stability, which, of course, unless you are completely funded by earned income, is tied to your ability to secure the support of a range of third-party payers. Thus, third-party payers will be central to any competitive strategy you decide to undertake.

In regard to your desired market position, ask the following questions:

- What financial resources will we need to achieve this position?
- Will it require more administrative capacity? More program staff? A new facility?
- How does our projected budget compare with our current year's?
- How confident are we about the stability of our current financial situation?
- What changes do we expect from our current third-party payers over the next few years?
- If we need more funding, where could we secure it? How likely is it that we could obtain it?
- If we want to grow, is acquisition of or partnering with a competitor a reasonable strategy for securing added capacity? Are we prepared for the significant financial and other resource requirements of implementing this strategy?

Selecting, Developing, and Implementing Your Strategies

Complete Worksheet 8.4 by starting with your desired market position, which you identified earlier. Then ask yourself the questions outlined in the decision tree diagram in Figure 8.1; your responses will help you sort through your third-party payer strategies. Make changes to the strategies you identified in Worksheet 8.4 as necessary, based on your responses to the questions in Figure 8.1.

Expanding Your Funding Base

If you will need significant additional funding to achieve your desired market position, consider how to expand your current funding base. You will need strong and positive relationships with your current third-party payers. In addition, you will need a solid list of potential third-party payers with whom you have or are developing positive relationships, as well as an aggressive strategy to cultivate them. You will need to consider a wide array of ways to increase your funding, including grants, contracts, donations, earned income from fees or ticket sales, income-producing ventures, and increased membership revenues, if that is an option.

In addition, one strategy you might consider is acquisition of or partnership with a competitor, if it would help you to achieve your desired market position and strengthen your financial condition. Be aware, however, that this is a resource-intensive strategy—one that requires significant time from board and staff members, as well as monetary resources to complete the deal.

The likelihood of your gaining the resources you need is not a static, once-and-for-all-time calculation. You can increase the likelihood of attracting resources by improving your competitive advantages, especially in relation to competitors that have secured those resources in the past. When you study your direct competitors and key indirect competitors, what do you learn? Why do they have contracts with a branch of local government that you do not? Why do they have one thousand individual donors, while you have one hundred? Why is their cost structure such that they actually produce a surplus from operations, while you find yourself offering the same program at a small loss each year? This sort of analysis can lead to both quick fixes and longer-term market insights that can yield a big payoff.

Basic Strategies to Strengthen Your Competitive Position

Regardless of which specific strategies you select in order to achieve your goals with third-party payers, there are some basic strategies that you should implement. Improving your organization's skills in various aspects of fundraising, such as proposal writing, prospect research, and personal solicitation, is a good idea, one that is feasible for most nonprofit fund seekers. Beyond skills, what sets the more successful seeker of funds apart from the pack?

WORKSHEET 8.4. IDENTIFYING FUNDING STRATEGIES BASED ON DESIRED MARKET POSITION AND PRESENT SITUATION.

1. Strategy regarding market position (Check one)	2. What funding will this require? (compared with the present level) (Check one)	3. How feasible is it to obtain the funding we need? (Check one)	4. How will we obtain the funding we need? (Check all that apply)	5. What do we need in addition to funding? (that is, what competitive advantages do we need?) (Check all that apply)
_____ Grow significantly (increase market share, expand into new markets) _____ Grow somewhat _____ Maintain current position _____ Exit/Shift _____ Assume niche _____ Other (specify)	_____ Significant increase _____ Moderate increase _____ Same level _____ Less _____ Other (specify)	_____ In hand _____ Very likely _____ Somewhat likely _____ Unlikely but possible _____ Unlikely _____ Other (specify)	_____ Seek funding from specific sources (list them) _____ Acquisition of or partnering with resource-rich market competitor that strengthens our position _____ Create sources of earned income (for example, fees, contracts) _____ Other (specify)	_____ Assess our outcomes and prove success _____ Improve our financial management and reporting _____ Improve our fundraising _____ Improve our communications _____ Other (specify)

Play to Win by David La Piana, ISBN 0-7879-6813-7, cloth, copyright © 2005 Jossey-Bass, An Imprint of Wiley.

FIGURE 8.1. DETERMINING FUNDING NEEDS TO ACHIEVE DESIRED MARKET POSITION.

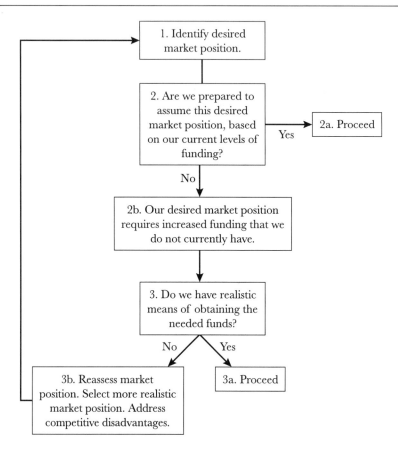

As I discussed earlier, the keys to success in attracting and retaining third-party payers are relationships, performance, and accountability. Some specific strategies that you can use to stand out from the competitive crowd on these critical dimensions and thus maximize your success in gaining third-party payer support include the following:

Demonstrate results. Assess your performance and document any particular strengths you identify. Benchmark these to the extent possible against others in the field, either locally or nationally. Once you have solid evidence that your performance is outstanding in some way (if indeed it is), you should not be shy about touting your successes. For example, if a nonprofit can claim, "Across the country only about 30 percent of serious juvenile offenders stay out of trouble after treatment; however, 75 percent of our clients do," third-party payers that are interested in juvenile justice issues will take notice; they will likely find this powerful and persuasive statement to be tremendously appealing. This organization could go further, trying to quantify dollars saved by its better-than-average performance: "The one hundred youths we successfully treat each year, at a cost of one million dollars, represent a savings of five million dollars in juvenile detention and court costs—a 500 percent payoff—in addition to the avoidance of pain and suffering for the youths, their families, and potential victims of youth crime." Not everyone cares about the lives of troubled youngsters, but presumably even the most hard-hearted among us wants to save public dollars and avoid becoming a crime victim!

Outcome measures, when contextualized within reasonable and valid benchmarks, are a strong selling point with many third-party payers. If you know your organization outperforms others in its field, you might urge third-party payers to conduct an evaluation of the field to see what outcomes are being achieved. You will also want to keep outcomes at the top of the list of topics discussed at meetings among third-party payers and service providers.

On the other hand, if your organization is not a top performer, you should first work to become one, within your current abilities, before trying this strategy. If you are concerned about your performance and are demonstrating concerted efforts to improve it, this too will reflect positively on your organization.

Build relationships when there is no money on the table. Wise nonprofit leaders build relationships with decision makers and decision influencers from third-party payer organizations at times when there is no money at stake. I offered a process for initiating these relationships earlier in this chapter. But there is always more that you can do. Attend dinners and events where such people might be present; try to write articles for local newspapers or professional journals that they might see; and otherwise cultivate business friendships. Develop relationships with your current and potential major individual donors. Take them to lunch. Host an event to recognize them and their contributions. Organize field trips to program sites for groups of board members and donors. In each case, ongoing efforts will mean that these relationships are in place when your organization needs to ask for support.

Be transparent. By all means, your organization should invest in a first-rate financial management and reporting system. This will provide the information that you need to make sound decisions and also generate the reports that you, the board, third-party payers, and others need. Stakeholders will appreciate the fact that your organization has provided this information without them having to ask for it and that when they do ask, it is readily available. A robust accounting system; timely, useful, easy-to-read financial reports; and competent accounting staff will provide your organization with a surprisingly effective management and communications tool. You will obtain a competitive advantage in the eyes of third-party payers, who are increasingly (and rightfully) concerned with accountability and transparency. Your financial management system should be used to develop financial status and performance reports in more detail, with greater frequency, and containing more useful information than others in the field.

With this approach to accounting, you promote a policy of "transparency plus." If it is not feasible to build this function in house, consider contracting out your financial management and reporting function to a professional firm that specializes in small business or nonprofit accounting. One way or another, you must have first-rate, timely information, presented in flexible formats to meet various needs.

Beyond the accounting function, it is important to cultivate transparency in all business dealings, including human resource management decisions. A competitive organization should practice full disclosure, as well as fair treatment of employees, vendors, and others. It is also critical that the organization cultivate a board of directors that provides independent oversight; the rubber-stamp nonprofit board must become obsolete.

Build relationships by serving as a source of information and assistance. Organizations should share useful or interesting information with their third-party payers, being sure, of course, not to violate confidentiality owed to someone else. Reliable information is difficult to come by, particularly for third-party payers, who regularly complain that they only tend to hear what the nonprofits they fund want them to hear. They yearn for, seek out, and value reliable sources of information. If you are identified as such a resource, you will stand out from the group of nonprofits in the same field that tends only to interact with funders when there is money on the table and only to communicate information that directly helps its own cause.

It is important that your organization's leaders never act self-servingly; doing so will undermine all their efforts to stand out. You and your colleagues should simply and generously offer your expertise, information, and advice. For example, if you learn of a funder in another part of the country who has just released a report that a local funder may be interested in, you can easily send an e-mail message to the local funder with a link to the on-line report.

From the foregoing discussion, you can see that successful competition for third-party payers is more about relationships than money. With everyone scrambling for dollars, the wise nonprofit leader presents herself as "above all that" and treats potential supporters as colleagues.

Assessing Your Outcomes

Just as you must assess the outcomes of your organization's programs and services, you must also assess the outcomes of your strategies for cultivating relationships with third-party payers and attaining your needed levels of funding. First, identify your specific strategies and the outcomes you expect. Periodically assess your performance against these desired outcomes. The most telling outcome will be whether you achieve your targeted level of funding, which is a quite concrete and easily assessable measure.

CHAPTER NINE

HUMAN RESOURCES

The goal of this chapter is to help you develop strategies that will make your organization more competitive in attracting a full array of human resources to support your mission. To achieve this goal, you must first understand the needs of your human resources (your staff, board members, and volunteers) and assess how well you are doing in meeting these needs. This assessment will allow you to identify your competitive advantages and disadvantages in relation to other organizations in your market or geographic area.

With the information from your assessment, you can set your human resource objectives, identifying potential strategies to address your competitive disadvantages and to promote your advantages. I will present basic strategies for attracting and keeping good people that all nonprofits should adopt, as well as strategies specific to your desired market position. With this foundation, you can determine which strategies are appropriate for your organization.

Who Are Your Human Resources?

Human resources is the catchall term for the people who are critical to your organization's governance, management, and work. In most staffed nonprofits, employees and contractors consume the largest portion of the budget. Moreover, board members and programmatic volunteers perform essential work for nonprofits. Finally, effective leadership, especially at the executive director level, is always critical and often in short supply. So my definition of human resources goes well beyond the usual meaning of "paid staff." You need to attract, orient, train, and motivate all of these people in order to succeed. And you must do all this amid keen competition from others who also want the benefit of the efforts of the best of them.

Several factors contribute to the competition for top talent at all organizational levels and for all roles. Many of the people you might like to hire, for example, could also work for the private sector or for government. These other sectors regularly compete with nonprofits for talented staff, typically paying higher wages and providing better benefits than most nonprofits can afford. As a result of this financial disadvantage, nonprofits compete for staff by emphasizing other factors—for example, an inspiring mission. Potential board members who can bring resources from their professional or social roles are also highly sought after. Nonprofits compete among themselves for board members by emphasizing their organization's accomplishments or leveraging a personal connection to the board candidate.

This chapter explores a variety of competitive strategies aimed at attracting and retaining the skilled board, staff, and volunteers your organization needs to perform its work, regardless of what market position you have now or aspire to secure in the future. The bottom line: in order to compete successfully for top talent, you need to be better than your competitors at meeting their needs.

Understanding the Needs of Your Staff, Board, and Volunteers

To attract and retain the staff, board, and volunteers that your organization needs to accomplish its work, you must understand these key stakeholders' needs. The needs of each group are similar in many respects, but they differ in some important ways. I will first discuss the common needs, then those that may be unique to each type of human resource.

Needs Common to All Groups

Some needs are shared by all people who might contribute to your organization in one way or another. These include the need to be part of an organization that

- Has an inspiring mission
- Has a good reputation
- Is effective at what it does

- Is financially stable
- Makes them feel needed and useful

Kouzes and Posner (2002, p. 25) provide a similar list of the attributes people seek in an organizational leader, based on extensive research.

Inspiring mission. Hopefully, everyone involved with your nonprofit is motivated by a commitment to the organization's work. A passionate attachment to mission is generally characteristic of those who work in the nonprofit sector, but some organizations are more effective than others at inspiring their people. If the mission is worth pursuing, it should be capable of inspiring everyone involved. This is as true for the receptionist as it is for board members.

Good reputation. To attract the best board members, staff, and volunteers, an organization must have a solid reputation for doing good work and operating in an ethical manner. It should be known in its community and its field for the quality of its work, the sound management of its financial resources, the positive attributes of its leadership, its values, and its ethics.

Effectiveness. It is not enough to have an inspiring mission and a positive reputation. An organization must deserve that reputation because it is effective at what it does. Reputation helps to attract people, but once they associate themselves with your organization, they will see for themselves whether it is indeed first-rate and ethical, and their contribution to your nonprofit's success will be at the level you need only if they find themselves part of a culture of effectiveness.

Financial stability. Financial stability is essential to your competitive success across all areas. While organizations can survive for a while on the basis of their mission and their past reputation, if they are financially unstable, it will eventually catch up with them. No one wants to work for, much less be on the board of an organization that is in financial trouble; this can be a huge competitive disadvantage in attracting and keeping people.

Providing feelings of being useful and needed. Often, nonprofit staff members work long hours for less compensation than they could receive elsewhere. Volunteers work for no pay at all. Board volunteers in particular are probably also donors: they pay to volunteer. To sustain this level of dedication, people need to feel that their presence each day at the organization is meaningful and important; otherwise, their sacrifices will not feel worthwhile.

Needs of Staff Members

Among your staff's needs are adequate pay and benefits. No one in your employ is looking to get rich, but everyone wants and deserves to live in some measure of comfort. The nonprofit sector is deeply rooted in a culture of volunteerism. In the past, many nonprofit staff members saw their work as quasi-volunteer in nature, so they subsidized their nonprofit employer by taking very low wages. This approach worked reasonably as recently as the 1970s, when most households were still supported by just one income. Women, especially highly educated and talented women, often working as underpaid or unpaid staff, were the backbone of the nonprofit sector.

As women began to enter the workforce in increasing numbers, this vital resource was drained from the nonprofit sector. Seniors, students, and other new volunteer resources have compensated in part for this tremendous loss, but there has not been enough of an increase in funding to adequately compensate paid staff. Salaries are often still at near-volunteer levels.

Despite the commitment of the nonprofit workforce (Light, 2002a), low compensation leads to high turnover, which results in resources being used up as organizations continually recruit and train new staff, all the while knowing that the best and brightest may well be short-timers. Once trained, these stars may be snatched up by the better-paying for-profit sector; they may shift to the public sector, which offers higher salaries and comprehensive benefits; they may be recruited to larger, more established nonprofits; or they may become consultants. This pattern is particularly common among younger staff members, who may be willing to sacrifice material comfort for a period of time but realize as they grow older that they may never be able to own a home or support a family on a nonprofit salary.

In order to attract and retain a top-notch staff, organizations must pay decent wages and provide sound benefits. Few nonprofits set out to pay substandard wages; they often simply lack the resources to do better. Increasingly, however, nonprofits are building their business models on business-comparable or market-rate compensation levels and are successfully attracting the resources to pay their staff members somewhat better. As I have mentioned before, success leads to more success. The organization that is continually struggling for adequate staffing will never reach its full potential in mission advancement. Sometimes, what is needed is a reconsideration of workload and staffing levels. One strategy is for the organization to decide to do less for a time and get by with fewer staff positions, using the savings to increase the remaining salaries.

Status and professional development are other top needs of staff members. Unlike the for-profit sector, there is generally much less emphasis on hierarchy among nonprofits. This is not to say that people do not value titles or office space; they do. But counterbalancing these values is an emphasis on meaningful work and continual professional development and growth. While smaller organizations may not be able to provide a career ladder with many steps, they can provide training, mentoring opportunities, and other forms of professional development such as tuition assistance. In most typically understaffed nonprofits, there should be no shortage of opportunities to broaden one's job or develop new skills. The key is to be creative in making these opportunities available to interested staff members.

Further, it is important to recognize the contributions of the staff. Just as they want to know that they are working for an organization that does good work, they want to be recognized for their own work and achievements. Too often, managers overlook this essential fact: people need to feel appreciated. An honest and heartfelt thank-you spoken publicly at a staff meeting, for example, can do wonders for morale.

In addition to these basic needs (competitive salary and benefits, status, professional development, and recognition), your staff likely has needs specific to your organization. These might be related to flexible work hours; the work environment and office space; access to computer equipment or other resources required to get their job done; management support; work culture (things like dress code or celebrations); and safety.

In order to learn about your staff's needs, you can conduct a survey that is similar to the customer and third-party payer research that I described earlier. Ask your staff what they like and don't like about their job, as well as what changes they would like to see. Here are some caveats to remember in conducting this research:

- Preserve confidentiality. The best way to do this is to have an outsider conduct the survey and summarize the findings. If it is not within your budget to hire a consultant, make sure there is a way for staff to submit their completed surveys anonymously.
- Keep the survey short and simple, but make sure to leave space for open-ended comments.
- Do not make promises you cannot keep; for example, do not promise that you will make requested changes unless you really will.
- Explain why you are conducting the survey—that you want to know their thoughts and concerns.
- Provide a summary of the findings. The best method is a short written report that is distributed and then discussed at a staff meeting. This gives you a chance to let staff know what you plan to do to address their concerns and provides time for you to respond to their questions. Be aware that staff members may not feel comfortable discussing issues in this forum. Another approach is to use smaller meetings with direct supervisors, if it makes sense, given your organization's size.

Conduct this survey periodically so that you can track changes over time. It is also a good way to assess the outcomes of any changes you make. In addition, routinely ask job applicants why they applied for a position with your organization. This is a great way to learn about the reputation of your organization and also to determine whether the applicant's expectations are realistic. Moreover, when employees leave your organization voluntarily, hold a standard exit interview and ask them why they are leaving.

Finally, one inventive way of getting feedback is to bring together the entire staff to meet with a facilitator, who asks them questions about their experience of the organization. The executive director and other senior managers are present but are not allowed to speak. They are there simply to listen to what their staff has to say, no matter how difficult it is to hear. After the meeting, the managers can review with the facilitator the meaning of what they have heard. This approach can only be undertaken when there is a fairly high degree of trust between staff and senior management. If there is any real or perceived retribution for speaking up, the whole effort will backfire.

Needs of Board Members

Board members give of themselves in many ways, for a variety of reasons. Similar to staff members and to other volunteers, they are drawn by the organization's mission and by their desire to be instrumental in furthering it. Just as you seek board members who are leaders, have good reputations, are successful in their work, and are well-connected in the community, board members seek organizations—and fellow board members—with these same attributes.

In most communities, demand for well-connected, smart, and influential board members far outstrips supply. Nonprofit boards of directors have never been asked to do as much as they are today. They must raise funds, provide strategic guidance, and keep a close, dispassionate eye on accountability issues and management's performance. Having the best people in these roles can make all the difference in an organization's ability to achieve success.

Board members need to feel that their time and expertise are being used effectively. In addition, because of their fiduciary responsibility, board members need to trust the staff leadership of the organization and know that the leadership is capable of succeeding.

To successfully perform their functions, board members also need to be oriented to the organization, and they need training for their roles and responsibilities. This training should be provided on an ongoing basis. To be effective ambassadors for your organization, board members must have a good understanding of its mission, vision, values, programs, customers, and staff and volunteers. They need current and accurate materials, such as case statements and talking points, to support them in this role. Most board members have many demands on their time, so you must use them efficiently. Meetings must be well organized and productive; committees must be well run and effective.

Finally, many board members are motivated to serve partly in order to foster their own network. They value the opportunity to make connections with other board members through their service. Like other volunteers, board members need to know that their contributions (time, expertise, and money) are appreciated and valued. Serving on a board should be enjoyable and rewarding.

To gain an understanding of how well your organization is meeting these needs of board members, I suggest periodically surveying them, the same as you do with staff. Many boards do this for themselves as part of an annual board self-evaluation process; this is better still.

Needs of Volunteers

Volunteers are the backbone of many nonprofits. Most organizations in the sector are operated entirely by volunteers; others depend to varying degrees on volunteer workers. Demanding work schedules, longer commutes, family commitments, and other factors are chipping away at the time people have available to volunteer. While there remain many potential volunteers in most communities, the supply is definitely smaller than the demand. Today's volunteers are highly selective; they seek to accomplish a lot through limited and flexible volunteer hours, including the following:

- *Gain skills and experience.* High school and college students, young adults, and reentry workers in particular may wish to leverage the experience gained from volunteering to help them in their job search.
- *Use their skills and expertise.* Older working and retired persons often want to give back to their community.
- *Participate in something that directly affects them, their family, and their community.* Examples include parents who volunteer at their children's school and community members who volunteer to improve their neighborhood park.
- *Do meaningful and fulfilling work.* In their work, volunteers have needs that are very similar to those of paid staff:

  - Receive adequate orientation and training
  - Be recognized and valued for their contributions
  - Work in a safe environment, with the resources they need to perform their work

As with your staff and board members, learn about your volunteers' needs by surveying them periodically. Ask them what they like about their volunteer work and what improvements they would like to see. All the caveats I mentioned earlier for surveys of your staff (such as keeping responses confidential, not making promises you cannot keep) apply equally to your volunteers. In addition to surveys, depending on how many volunteers you have, it can be helpful to conduct focus groups. These sessions allow volunteers to brainstorm on solutions in areas of concern. The face-to-face setting also helps volunteers to feel that they are being heard and connects them to the organization in a new and different way.

Your Organization's Objectives: What Do You Want to Achieve?

In this section, you will consider your organization's objectives. Obviously, the starting point is your current position. Just as you did earlier for your customers and your third-party payers, begin by trying to understand how well your organization is meeting the needs of your staff, board members, and volunteers.

Start by drawing on your own experience and feedback from the surveys and focus groups discussed in the previous section. Complete Worksheet 9.1, assessing your organization's competitive advantages in the areas listed in the second column.

Assess Your Current Position

Your responses to Worksheet 9.1 will give you an overall sense of how well you currently meet the needs of your staff, board members, and volunteers. The areas in which you gave your organization a "1" are those in which you have a competitive advantage; those in which you gave your organization a "3" are areas of competitive disadvantage. In the next section, you will draw on this information to determine your current position regarding the attraction and retention of people.

Compare Your Organization with Competitors

Now that you have a better understanding of your competitive advantages and disadvantages in human resources, compare your organization with your competitors to determine your current position. Fill in Worksheet 9.2 by drawing on the competitor analyses you completed in Chapter Six (Worksheet 6.1). Specifically, examine those you identified as having competitive advantages related to human resources. Include direct, substitutable, and indirect competitors. To fill in

WORKSHEET 9.1. ASSESSMENT OF COMPETITIVE ADVANTAGES AND DISADVANTAGES IN HUMAN RESOURCES.

Type of Human Resource	Attribute	Competitive Advantage or Disadvantage (check only one)		
		Competitive Advantage (1)	Neutral (neither an advantage nor a disadvantage) (2)	Competitive Disadvantage (3)
All (staff, volunteers, board)	Mission	_____ Compelling (1)	_____ Lukewarm (2)	_____ Not compelling (3)
	Reputation	_____ Excellent (1)	_____ Fair (2)	_____ Poor (3)
	Perception of outcomes	_____ Positive (1)	_____ Neutral (2)	_____ Negative (3)
	Financial stability	_____ Excellent (1)	_____ Fair (2)	_____ Poor (3)
Staff	Salary	_____ Competitive (1)	_____ Midrange (2)	_____ Low-end (3)
	Fringe benefits	_____ Competitive (1)	_____ Midrange (2)	_____ Low-end (3)
	Professional development	_____ Excellent (1) (We do this well)	_____ Fair (2)	_____ Poor (3) (We do not offer much in this area)
	Recognition and rewards	_____ Excellent (1) (We do this well)	_____ Fair (2) (We do this to some extent)	_____ Poor (3) (We do not do this well or consistently)
	Access to resources to get work done (for example, computer, phone, Internet access, work space, e-mail, materials)	_____ Excellent (1) (We provide all needed resources)	_____ Fair (2) (We provide most needed resources)	_____ Poor (3) (We are limited in this area)

Play to Win by David La Piana, ISBN 0-7879-6813-7, cloth, copyright © 2005 Jossey-Bass, An Imprint of Wiley.

Type of Human Resource	Attribute	Competitive Advantage (1)	Competitive Advantage or Disadvantage (check only one)	
			Neutral (neither an advantage nor a disadvantage) (2)	Competitive Disadvantage (3)
	Training and orientation	_____ Excellent (1) (We do this well)	_____ Fair (2)	_____ Poor (3) (We do not offer much in this area)
	Morale and satisfaction with work	_____ Excellent (1)	_____ Fair (2)	_____ Poor (3)
Volunteers	Professional development	_____ Excellent (1) (We do this well)	_____ Fair (2)	_____ Poor (3) (We do not offer much in this area)
	Recognition and rewards	_____ Excellent (1) (We do this well)	_____ Fair (2) (We do this to some extent)	_____ Poor (3) (We do not do this well or consistently)
	Access to resources to get work done (for example, computer, phone, Internet access, work space, e-mail, materials)	_____ Excellent (1) (We provide all needed resources)	_____ Fair (2) (We provide most needed resources)	_____ Poor (3) (We are limited in this area)
	Training and orientation	_____ Excellent (1) (We do this well)	_____ Fair (2)	_____ Poor (3) (We do not offer much in this area)

(Continued)

Play to Win by David La Piana, ISBN 0-7879-6813-7, cloth, copyright © 2005 Jossey-Bass, An Imprint of Wiley.

WORKSHEET 9.1. ASSESSMENT OF COMPETITIVE ADVANTAGES AND DISADVANTAGES IN HUMAN RESOURCES (*CONTINUED*).

Type of Human Resource	Attribute	Competitive Advantage or Disadvantage (*check only one*)		
		Competitive Advantage (1)	Neutral (neither an advantage nor a disadvantage) (2)	Competitive Disadvantage (3)
	Morale and satisfaction with work	_____ Excellent (1)	_____ Fair (2)	_____ Poor (3)
Board Members	Access to information needed to get work done	_____ Excellent (1) (We provide all needed information)	_____ Fair (2) (We provide most needed information)	_____ Poor (3) (We are limited in this area)
	Training and orientation	_____ Excellent (1) (We do this well)	_____ Fair (2)	_____ Poor (3) (We do not offer much in this area)
	Morale and satisfaction with work	_____ Excellent (1)	_____ Fair (2)	_____ Poor (3)
	Networking and camaraderie	_____ Excellent (1)	_____ Fair (2)	_____ Poor (3)

Play to Win by David La Piana, ISBN 0-7879-6813-7, cloth, copyright © 2005 Jossey-Bass, An Imprint of Wiley.

WORKSHEET 9.2. ORGANIZATIONS WITH COMPETITIVE ADVANTAGES IN HUMAN RESOURCES.

Competitor	Type of Competitor (direct, substitutable, indirect)	Competitors with Advantages in Attracting and Keeping Talent (check areas of competitive advantage over your organization)				Comments
		Board	Executive Director	Staff	Volunteers	

Play to Win by David La Piana, ISBN 0-7879-6813-7, cloth, copyright © 2005 Jossey-Bass, An Imprint of Wiley.

the "Comments" column, consider what you can learn from each competitor. Do any of your competitors have specific advantages in human resources? What can you learn from them?

When completed by you and your market research team, Worksheets 9.1 and 9.2 help you to understand your organization's relative competitiveness for human resources. Ask the following questions: Are we in a strong position to compete for board members, staff, and volunteers because on balance, we have many competitive advantages? Are we in the middle of the pack? Or do our competitive disadvantages outweigh our advantages relative to other competitors?

Choose Your Desired Market Position

In Chapter Seven, I discussed the three primary choices for your organization's overall competitive and market position. You will recall that you can choose to do one of the following:

- Improve your market position by expanding your market share
- Maintain your market position and market share
- Shift, diversify, or remove your organization from the market

Regardless of the market position you seek, your success depends in large part on your ability to attract and keep top-notch people of all kinds. Strong organizations attract the best people and, as a result, become even stronger—the virtuous cycle once again. To be successful in securing and maintaining any market position, your organization must have a compelling mission, a sound reputation, effective programs, and financial stability, and its people must feel useful and valued. Your first step must be to address any competitive disadvantages in these critical areas. This may involve putting other priorities aside for a time while you focus on changing disadvantages into advantages. Only after you have done this can you consider an expansion strategy. To attempt growth with a weak board or an inadequate staff is to invite disaster.

Your strategies for competing for board members, executives, staff members, and volunteers are interrelated with your overall market position strategies. For example, if you seek to expand, you will most likely need additional program staff, and you may need to increase your management staffing to supervise them. You may desire a greater number of volunteers. Your board may even decide to expand its size in order to be representative of a larger number of constituents or to find an executive with experience in running a larger operation.

If you seek to maintain your current market position, you will still need to evaluate your competitiveness and develop strategies for ongoing recruitment and replacement of people in each category whom you will lose through normal attrition.

If you seek to shift focus or diversify, you may need to retrain your staff or even attract a different mix of skills and expertise at the management or line level. A retrenchment and niche strategy may require a staff that is more highly focused on doing one thing exceedingly well.

How do you determine your human resource strategies? Obviously, you must first begin with the larger question: Where are we going? Once you know your desired market position, you can develop aligned strategies for attracting the best people to help you get there. A good starting point is to determine which areas are currently competitive advantages and which are competitive disadvantages for your organization when it comes to attracting the best people and keeping them involved. You can do this most readily by examining Worksheets 9.1 and 9.2. For ease of review, summarize your findings on Worksheet 9.3.

If it turns out that you are a relatively strong competitor, this will support your movement toward your desired market position, whatever it may be. A weaker competitor may find it hard to recruit the board it needs, for example, to complete a major building program or the executive director it needs to become the leader in its field. First addressing any major competitive disadvantages will improve your chances of successfully reaching your desired market position.

Selecting, Developing, and Implementing Your Strategies

Complete Worksheet 9.4 to identify strategies that will attract the people you need in order to secure the market position you desire. First, fill in the market position you seek. Then, consider what this means for your human resource needs. For example, do you need a better-connected board in order to expand? Or do you need to downsize staff while you work on financial stability?

Do your people lack specific skills or expertise? For example, if your financial situation is unstable, you may need board members with strong fundraising or business skills. If you plan to change your program emphasis, you may need staff and volunteers with different expertise.

The fourth column of Worksheet 9.4 requires you to consider how you will meet your organizational needs for human resources. Should you mount an all-out recruitment effort? Do you need to train existing staff? Do you need to better meet the needs of your current staff and volunteers for professional development, recognition, salary, benefits, or resources to get their jobs done?

Realistically, almost all of these strategies require some financial resources in order to be implemented. Some require more than others. In selecting strategies,

WORKSHEET 9.3. SUMMARY OF COMPETITIVE ADVANTAGES AND DISADVANTAGES IN HUMAN RESOURCES.

Area of Competitive Advantage or Disadvantage in Attracting and Retaining People	Advantage?	Disadvantage?	Comments

WORKSHEET 9.4. SELECTING AND DEVELOPING YOUR HUMAN RESOURCE STRATEGIES.

Desired Market Position (write in what you seek to achieve)	What does your organization need to do to achieve this position?		Possible Strategies (what you need to do to achieve your desired position)	Competitive Advantages That Will Help with This Strategy
	Need for More/Fewer People (check off and circle)	**Need for Specific Types of People (skills needed)**		
	_____ Change number of board members. Explain: _____ _____ _____	_____ Need to strengthen board in (write in): _____ _____ _____	_____ Recruit (circle all that apply) Board members Executive director Staff Volunteers	Compelling mission, great reputation, financial stability, strong leadership, high morale
	_____ Change number of staff. Explain: _____ _____ _____	_____ Need to strengthen executive director in (write in): _____ _____ _____	_____ Provide training for (circle all that apply) Board members Executive director Staff Volunteers Specify:	Experienced trainers on staff, board
	_____ Change number of volunteers. Explain: _____ _____ _____	_____ Need to strengthen staff in (write in): _____ _____ _____	_____ Implement recognition or rewards program for (circle all that apply) Staff Volunteers Comments:	History with successful recognition efforts
		_____ Need to strengthen volunteers in (write in): _____ _____ _____	_____ Improve salary for (circle all that apply) Executive director Staff Comments:	Strong income capacity, strong case for increasing salary to improve competitive position
			_____ Improve benefits for (circle all that apply) Executive director Staff Comments:	Strong income capacity, strong case for increasing benefits to improve competitive position
			_____ Address resource needs of (circle all that apply) Board Executive director Staff Volunteers Comments:	

you will need to determine whether you have the time and financial resources to implement them. For example, if your desired position entails growth, and you require more staff but lack the financial resources to hire them, does your organization have current staff whose skills are being underutilized who might jump at an opportunity to expand their work? Perhaps you have the ability to hire staff but cannot pay competitively. Here you could promote your competitive advantages, which might include an excellent reputation, opportunities for professional development, advancement opportunities due to anticipated growth, flexible work hours, or opportunities to work with recognized leaders in the field who will serve as mentors.

Other strategies can enhance your competitiveness by addressing your people's needs without spending money. Here are some examples related to staff, drawn from my own experience:

Titles. Some organizations treat titles as if they had inherent value; they do not. A senior social worker in one organization has less authority for independent action and makes less money than a "mere" counselor in another. As an executive director, my attitude was that staff could have any title they wanted, except mine. Sometimes an upgraded title can be more satisfying than a small pay raise. Titles are also important to volunteers. Print business cards, give them reasonable titles, and they will appreciate the recognition.

Office space. Size and location of work space are important status symbols in many nonprofits. You could give everyone what they want, but it might be difficult to find a building with fifty corner offices! As an executive director, I encountered a situation where our senior management team outgrew our office space on the second floor. A battle ensued over which of the senior staff would take a lesser office on the first floor with the program people. This argument rose to silly proportions and began to have a negative impact on the morale of the line staff, who were, after all, located downstairs and who for the most part had no office whatsoever. I decided that the best thing to do was to move myself downstairs. I put a desk in the back of the reception area, behind the secretaries. This was referred to as "moving the throne" and caused the management team to see the silliness of their battle. Through my greater proximity to the action, it also gave me an education in the daily work of the organization. Be creative; you never know what might work.

Career counseling. Paradoxically, I found that one of the most effective ways to keep staff for the long term was to build in to their annual performance review the question "What do you want to do next?" Rather than pretending that people have no aspirations beyond their current job, this approach opened a dialogue between staff members and their supervisors. In some cases, if someone wanted to return to school to upgrade their skills, we helped, later rehiring the person in a new position after he or she had completed a degree. Other staff members confessed to wanting to go into real estate or some other endeavor. We encouraged them to do so, offering advice and even contacts in the desired field, and in this way built their loyalty and trust. Over time, our turnover dropped.

If your objective is to maintain your current market position, consider what you need to do to remain where you are. While you may not need to expand staffing, you should still address any areas in which your analysis found your organization lacking. Addressing competitive disadvantages may include implementing a more competitive salary and benefits package over time, improving opportunities for professional development, addressing leadership weaknesses, or achieving higher levels of satisfaction (improving morale) among your staff, board members, and volunteers.

If your objective involves downsizing, a niche, diversifying, or shifting your focus, your organization may need to train staff and volunteers to perform new roles and to assume new responsibilities. It will require training everyone in the new message that they should communicate about your organization, so that they can effectively perform as spokespersons and fundraisers.

Assessing Your Outcomes

Just as you assessed the outcomes of your strategies for competing successfully for third-party payers in Chapter Eight, you need to assess the outcomes of your strategies related to human resources. Periodically assess your performance against your desired outcomes. Set timeframes for reviewing your achievements. At these points, compare your actual outcomes to your target outcomes, and determine what changes you need to make when you do not achieve your targets. Keep working at your human resource challenges; for you as a nonprofit leader, people are your most critical asset.

CHAPTER TEN

THE MEDIA AND THE PUBLIC AT LARGE

The primary goal of this chapter is to help you develop strategies to obtain the attention and recognition you desire from the media and the public. The media and the public are important resources for your organization in its quest to secure its desired market position.

To achieve this goal, you will follow the same steps as in the previous chapters in Part Three. The strategies you develop have as their foundation an exchange relationship providing benefit to all parties involved. In the case of the media, you provide information that reporters and editors need to meet the demands of their constituents (their readers, viewers, listeners, subscribers, and advertisers), and ideally, they provide your organization with positive publicity. The primary constituent of the general media is the public. Thus, you reach the public through the media. You can also reach the public in other ways, including public relations efforts, which I will discuss briefly as well.

The starting point for your media and public relations efforts is an understanding of who these media and the public are. In order to gain the attention of the media and, in turn, the public and to secure the support your organization needs from them, you first need to understand their needs. By meeting these needs, you will develop positive relationships. Considering the various ways in which the media and the general public can help your organization, it is a good idea to develop strategies to build a positive relationship with them. The final steps are to identify, develop, and implement your strategies and monitor them over time to ensure that they support the overall market position you seek. Remember, media attention to the nonprofit sector is limited and hotly contested, so you will have to compete for it.

Who Are the Media and the Public at Large?

By "the media," I mean forms of communication that depend on radio, television, newspapers, magazines, and the Internet. Depending on your market, the relevant media may be local, regional, statewide, national, or possibly international. For most organizations, the primary relevant media are local and regional; therefore, I will focus this discussion on that level of coverage. This will provide a good foundation for strategies relating to any level of media that you target. Similarly, when speaking of the general public, I will focus primarily on local and regional communities.

The media can be very important to your organization. Positive publicity— whether in the form of a newspaper article, a public service announcement on television or radio, an on-air interview, or an article in a trade publication—is a valuable resource for any organization. Strategies for reaching the media and the public are integrally related. The media want stories that are of interest to the public, and they also shape public opinion.

While you have control over the messages you print in your marketing materials, post on your Web site, and deliver through your spokespersons, you have much less control over the media. This is a double-edged sword. Because organizations do not control the media, what is reported tends to have much more credibility than, say, your own marketing materials. Further, the media have a much greater reach than the typical nonprofit can possibly achieve through its own marketing and communications function; that is, newspapers, radio, and television are probably read, heard, and viewed by many more people than are your marketing materials. Therefore, the media not only have higher credibility, they also have an impact on significant numbers of people. The result: a positive article in your local paper can be far more valuable—and much less costly—in generating support for your organization than an expensive marketing brochure.

On the other hand, negative publicity—for example, a story portraying your organization as wasteful—can do great damage. Even if the story contains erroneous information, it may be next to impossible to undo the damage after it is out. At a minimum, your damage control efforts will divert valuable staff and board resources from focusing on achieving a competitive market position. Therefore, negative publicity and its detrimental impact on the public's perception of your organization are to be avoided at all costs.

"The public" is a somewhat nebulous concept. In one sense, it includes every-one in your market or community. From your point of view, however, it includes all who might in some way be affected by or who might themselves affect your organization. "The public" is also one step removed from those who are directly affected by your organization—your customers, funders, partners, and members. While these constituents are close to your organization—and so should receive internal communications and not be dependent primarily on the general media for their information—they are still affected by the media and anything reported about your organization, its competitors, and general trends in your field.

Among those directly affected by your organization are your competitors. Their perceptions will be to some extent shaped by the media, which will influ-ence their actions. For example, a competitor who perceives your organization as stronger than itself in one area may be encouraged to withdraw from that por-tion of the market because it believes your organization can better meet customers' needs, has better funding, and is so securely ensconced that it will not be able to compete with you. The opposite is also true. If a competitor believes you to be weak, it may see this as an opportunity to move into your market, seeking to lure away your staff, board members, customers, or third-party payers. So beware of a poor public perception, and cultivate effective media strategies.

While you cannot control the media or public opinion, you can do much to influence them. This chapter helps you develop strategies for achieving a positive relationship with the media and the public.

Understanding the Needs of the Media and the Public

The needs of the media and the public are similar and interrelated. The media intend to serve the public's interest—that is, to provide information that the pub-lic is interested in and needs to know. While some media, such as a community newspaper or local radio news show, seek to serve the public in general, most media target a segment of the public that may have specific interests. It is also important to understand that the media are themselves highly competitive. As a result, reporters are interested in stories that make a big splash. Scandals seem to sell more newspapers and attract more television ads than do human interest stories, and journalists are trained to be skeptical of people with a story to tell, so most reporters love to latch onto a juicy feature, regardless of the consequences for your organization.

To understand the needs of the media as they relate to your organization, you must know which segments are potentially most interested in your work. Then you must determine which of these are of most interest to you. Since your goal is to achieve awareness and a positive perception in the minds of constituents so that you will gain their support, you need to consider which media best reach your target audiences. Complete Worksheet 10.1 by drawing on your knowledge and experience, as well as the findings of the surveys and other market research that you have conducted. In this way, you can learn about the media that best reach your current and potential customers, funders, human resources, and other constituents, such as potential donors.

Having identified the media that target your organization's intended audiences, you can focus on their specific interests as you develop your strategies for gaining their attention. Much has been written on how to gain positive publicity, and it is beyond the scope of this book to repeat that information here. I will summarize the key points as they relate to developing competitive strategies.

The basic need of the media is for stories that are pertinent and of interest to their target audiences. Editors and reporters are very busy people. They appreciate organizations that are proactive in understanding their needs and interests and that provide them with timely and accurate information that will appeal to their audiences' interests. They want sources that they can trust to meet these criteria. They also want information to be provided to them in an easy-to-access manner (usually via e-mail or fax) and for any supplemental information such as background information on your organization and photos to be easily accessible.

The public has an interest in knowing about organizations that operate in the community and about the impact of these programs on the community. All of those touched by your organization—either now or possibly in the future—have a need to know about you.

Following this quick overview of the needs of the media and the public, it's time to develop your specific objectives in this area. As you identify your objectives and your strategies to achieve them, you will deepen your understanding of these important resources.

Your Organization's Objectives: What Do You Want to Achieve?

To develop strategies for cultivating the positive support of the media and the public, you need to understand your current position with them. Drawing on the research you conducted in previous chapters and on your organization's experience, respond to the statements in Worksheet 10.2. These statements are indicators of strength and possible competitive advantage regarding the media and the public.

Any statements in Worksheet 10.2 that you disagree with represent areas of competitive disadvantage, because you can be certain that other nonprofits in your

WORKSHEET 10.1. CHARACTERISTICS AND MEDIA INTERESTS OF CONSTITUENTS.

Constituent Segment	Characteristics (demographics)	Media (Indicate primary medium for each constituent segment)	Specific Media (Name a media outlet)
Current and potential customers (include direct and indirect customers):	What are their characteristics? • Age and gender • Socioeconomic background • Race or ethnicity • Languages spoken • Geographic location	Radio stations listened to Local television stations viewed Community papers read Community Web sites visited Community billboards Community meetings attended Trade publications read	
Funders (include foundations, corporations, government agencies):	Characteristics:	Community papers read Trade publications read Other key media	
Major donors:	Characteristics:	Radio stations listened to Local television stations viewed Community papers read Community Web sites visited Community billboards Community meetings attended Trade publications read	

Play to Win by David La Piana, ISBN 0-7879-6813-7, cloth, copyright © 2005 Jossey-Bass, An Imprint of Wiley.

Members (if applicable):	Characteristics:	Radio stations listened to Local television stations viewed Community papers read Community Web sites visited Community billboards Community meetings attended Trade publications read
Policymakers and community leaders:	Characteristics:	Radio stations listened to Local television stations viewed Community papers read Community Web sites visited Community billboards Community meetings attended Trade publications read
Competitors and partners:	Characteristics:	Radio stations listened to Local television stations viewed Community papers read Community meetings attended Trade publications read
General public	Characteristics:	Radio stations listened to Local television stations watched Community papers read Community Web sites visited Community billboards Community meetings attended Trade publications read

WORKSHEET 10.2. ASSESSMENT OF COMPETITIVE ADVANTAGES IN MEDIA AND PUBLIC RELATIONS.

Indicators of Strength and Competitive Advantage with Respect to Media and Public Relations	Do you agree with the statement? Is it true for your organization?				
	Agree	Somewhat Agree	Disagree	Don't Know	Not Applicable
Media and public relations function					
We have formal policies (for example, a designated media contact person) that address routine communication with media such as general media inquiries, requests for interviews, and when critical issues/crises arise.					
Board members understand their role as spokespersons for our organization and effectively represent it in the community.					
Our staff and board members are aware of and adhere to our media relations policies and strategies.					
Our executive director, key staff, and board members spend sufficient time developing relationships with community leaders and the media.					
We provide regular updates to our constituents on our activities that are of interest and value to them.					
Outcomes of media and public relations functions					
Media: We have good working relationships with representatives of the media.					
Media: Our organization is seen as a resource by the media.					

Play to Win by David La Piana, ISBN 0-7879-6813-7, cloth, copyright © 2005 Jossey-Bass, An Imprint of Wiley.

Statement					
Media: Our organization receives frequent favorable coverage in local and regional media.					
Public: Our organization is well known and well respected in the community.					
Public: Our stakeholders (customers, constituents, the general public) know and understand the value of our work.					
Resources in support of media and public relations: Staff and board expertise and time allocation					
We have the right skills and sufficient resources of staff and board expertise and time to effectively perform necessary media and public relations functions.					
Resources in support of media and public relations: Market research					
We know who our primary stakeholders and constituents are and how to communicate with them (which media to use).					
We know enough about the community and the constituents we serve.					
We know about trends within and outside our community that may affect our organization and our work.					
We understand the value of our programs to our community.					
Resources in support of media and public relations: Marketing and communications					
Our Web site is well designed, current, and frequently updated.					
Our marketing materials are consistent in content and look (branding); they clearly identify our organization.					
Our marketing messages are consistent, clear, easy to understand, and supportive of our mission, vision, and values.					

market are effectively meeting these requirements. By identifying your competitive advantages and disadvantages, you can get a sense of your position in the struggle for media and public attention. Your strategies related to the media and the public should be designed to achieve sound outcomes that are appropriate for your organization's situation. For some grassroots or niche organizations, it may not be realistic to achieve frequent, favorable media coverage. However, there are other outcomes that represent a strong competitive position with the media, such as having positive relationships with key media representatives.

Next, examine your competitors, including any indirect competitors that always seem to get great publicity in your community. What can you learn from their advantages in the area of media and public relations? Which competitors get positive media coverage? What types of stories are reported? Do your competitors have effective spokespersons who are frequently called upon to give their opinion on topics of community interest? Who are these spokespersons, and what can you learn from them? Do competitor organizations hold community events that receive good media coverage? Do they hold press conferences, media briefings, or other media events? What staff do they have to support their media and public relations efforts? Which competitors have effectively handled crisis situations? Do additional research to find out what makes organizations effective in media and public relations.

Now, taking what you have learned from your analyses in Worksheet 10.2, complete Worksheet 10.3 to create a summary snapshot of your current competitive position in media and public relations. What changes could you make to improve your current situation? Insert your ideas in the right column of Worksheet 10.3.

If your outcomes are poor, you will definitely want to make some changes. Regardless of what overall market position you seek, you will need the aid of good media and public relations. To improve your position, you will need to consider your budget and how feasible it will be to gain greater public awareness, given the resources you have and the nature of your organization's work. Some organizations will have broad appeal because they have a simple-to-grasp concept or an instantly appealing target population. Other organizations will need to focus on a specific segment of the media and the public that they have identified as already having an interest in—or related to—their mission.

Ideally, your media and public relations activities would produce frequent positive publicity; solid relationships with media representatives; and the ability to be viewed as an expert and a reliable source for news. Your activities should also help your organization to become well known to the general public as a valuable community resource and within your specific subsector as a model organization. Achieving these results requires a significant investment of time on the part of skilled staff

WORKSHEET 10.3. CURRENT AND DESIRED POSITION
IN MEDIA AND PUBLIC RELATIONS.

Indicators of Competitive Advantage	Current Position (check one)			Desired Position (How can you improve your position?)
	Excellent	**Fair**	**Poor**	
Media relations function				
Public relations function				
Media relations outcomes				
Public relations outcomes				
Resources: Staff and board expertise and time allocated to media and public relations				
Resources: Market research function				
Resources: Marketing and communications function				

and board members. The magnitude of your public and media relations activities will depend on your market, your available resources, and your desired market position. A growth orientation, for example, will be aided by a higher profile.

If your organization has limited resources, a more viable approach may be a targeted rather than a broad effort. The objective might be to obtain periodic favorable media coverage in specific media that reach your organization's primary target audiences, to avoid any negative coverage, and to gain positive public awareness in key segments of the community that represent your primary target audiences and constituents.

While I generally recommend that organizations seek positive media and public attention, there are definitely times when you may not want such visibility. For example, if your organization is experiencing a crisis such as financial instability, low morale, or the unplanned departure of key leadership, this is not the time to draw attention to yourself. In these instances, "flying under the radar" and crisis management may be your best strategies until you are able to remedy the situation. At a minimum, however, you will need a plan in place to handle media and public inquiries.

Selecting, Developing, and Implementing Your Strategies

To achieve your media and public awareness objectives, you will need effective strategies. The strategies suggested in this section start with the basics, which every organization should employ, regardless of what market position it seeks, then move on to more specific strategies to support the move toward your desired market position.

Develop a market and competitor research capacity. Regardless of your desired market position, you need key information about your market, including customers, third-party payers, board members, staff, volunteers, competitors, partners, and the general public in your community. If as you worked your way through Part Two you did not develop at least a basic market and competitor research function, consider some simple processes to collect and analyze information that will help you understand your market position and value to your constituents. These processes should be maintained, so that trends can be monitored and your information remains current. Often you can recruit college students majoring in marketing or communications to help out. There may also be a program in nonprofit management nearby that would welcome the opportunity to offer its students this field experience. If nothing else, I hope that I have convinced you of the value of good market and competitor research.

Develop knowledge of your local media. Whether your desired outcome is to be relatively unnoticed or on the front page, you still need to know the key media that reach your constituents. Based on your understanding of your constituents and the media that reach them—including newspaper, radio and television stations, Internet sites, trade publications, and community events—identify the constituents with which you need visibility. Draw on your competitor research. Where do they get their stories placed?

As with market research, you can often find students to help with this type of basic research. At a minimum, you need an understanding of how to work with the media. Knowing your market will provide a good foundation. Recruit a board member who works in media or public relations. Make sure that internal stakeholders have consistent information so they can present a consistent message.

Track your media coverage. Put copies of articles in your marketing packet and on your Web site; good publicity is the best marketing tool you can have. Share articles with your third-party payers. If you are a membership organization, include them in your member newsletter. Some organizations use a clipping service to track media coverage. However, simply enlisting your board and staff in scanning your local papers and news broadcasts is usually sufficient. The Internet is a great tool for this research, too.

Build relationships with local media representatives. With a basic understanding of the media you want to target, identify reporters who are interested in the type of information and stories that your nonprofit might provide. Read bylines for the names of journalists who write on related topics. Find out as much as you can about them, including whether they have daily, weekly, or monthly deadlines. Send them press releases when your organization has something timely to report. Follow up your press release with a call to the reporter to pitch your story, making sure to emphasize why you think she will be interested and why the story is newsworthy.

Make sure the relationship goes both ways. Do not contact reporters only when you want your story published. Send them information that may be helpful. Seek to become a knowledge expert whom they feel comfortable calling when they need a good quote. Always respond quickly to their requests, and be sure the information you provide is accurate. If you do not know the answer to a question, be honest. Try to find a source that can help them.

If you have something to say on a topic of interest to newspaper readers, consider submitting a letter to the editor or an op-ed piece. This is another way to establish your organization's leaders as experts and to educate the public about a topic.

The degree to which you pursue this strategy will depend on the resources that you have available and on your desired market position. If you are seeking to expand within your market or are striving to maintain your position in a highly competitive market, you may want more media coverage than if you are withdrawing from some part of a market.

Launch a campaign to achieve high visibility. This is a strategy for nonprofits with strong competitive advantages that are seeking to maintain or expand their market position. Before you embark on this path, do your research; know your market well. Be prepared to highlight your competitive advantages without disparaging your competitors. Groom your leaders to be knowledge experts. Develop relationships with the media, and know the topics of greatest interest to their target audiences—which are yours as well.

If you launch a proactive strategy to achieve high visibility, you should include several of the approaches described earlier, such as issuing press releases; writing op-ed pieces for newspapers; providing speakers through a speakers bureau; holding press conferences or staging media events; or providing leaders to serve as knowledge experts, offering helpful information to the media and making themselves available for an interview when a quote is needed to round out a story.

If you are in a niche market, your strategies may be more focused. For example, you may target alternative, independent, or specialized media and extremely specific segments of the public (for example, a nonprofit that advocates for bicycling to work would want coverage by bicycling magazines).

Use a change to attract attention. Organizational change—a merger, a shift in focus, a new leader, or the opening of a new program or building—offers an opportunity to gain public visibility through the media. If you are planning a major change of this nature, this is a great time to build general awareness of your organization while highlighting positive aspects of the change. Make sure that your board, staff, and volunteers are apprised of the change and its value prior to going public.

When other organizations are involved—for example, in a new partnership—make sure to coordinate media efforts with them. It is well worth the time spent to ensure a consistent message. Also, consider holding a press conference to announce the change. It gives you more control over the information and gives reporters time to clarify any ambiguities.

Use community relations to build awareness. Community relations activities offer a way around the media to get your organization's information directly out to the community. These activities include having a presence at public meetings and at community events such as arts festivals, street fairs, picnics, and holiday celebrations. These are opportunities to directly reach a wide cross section of people in an informal and welcoming environment. Examples include a health clinic that provides free blood pressure screenings at the city's annual health fair and a museum that offers a free admission day for families on selected holidays. Having your spokespersons as featured speakers at community events is another way to gain visibility.

Strategy summary. Worksheet 10.4 displays the strategies that I have just discussed. Examine it, and select the strategies that will best support your organization in attaining its desired market position with the help of the media and the

WORKSHEET 10.4. DEVELOPING AND IMPLEMENTING STRATEGIES FOR ACHIEVING YOUR DESIRED POSITION.

Column 1 Determining Your Strategies (Enter your response to the statement below in Column 2.)	Column 2 Response to statement in Column 1 (check one)			Column 3 Plan for Developing and Implementing the Strategy (Complete this section if your response to Column 2 is "Somewhat Agree" or "Disagree")			
	Agree	Somewhat Agree	Disagree	Activities (Example activities are in italics. Note that the first two strategies are recommended for all organizations. These are market research and media research. Others are optional.)	Responsible Persons Examples	Resources Needed Examples	Time-frame
Market research capacity: We have a solid market research capacity that informs us of the needs and characteristics of our constituents (including current and potential customers, human resources, third-party payers, members, community leaders, and the public).				Review Part Two, Chapters Four and Five, to identify activities to develop this capacity.	*Consider student interns to assist*	*Internet access*	
Media research capacity: We have a solid media research capacity. We know which media reach our constituents and the names of reporters and editors.				• *Review market research findings* • *Identify preferred sources of news or information and preferred reporters* • *Track coverage*	*Consider student interns to assist*	*Internet access*	
Media relations: We have positive relationships with representatives of the media.				We want to focus on improving our relationships with the media now. We will (list activities) • *Develop media list* • *Provide information to reporters* • *and so on*	*Communi-cations coordina-tor*	*Board and executive spokesper-sons, staff time and expertise*	

(Continued)

Play to Win by David La Piana, ISBN 0-7879-6813-7, cloth, copyright © 2005 Jossey-Bass, An Imprint of Wiley.

WORKSHEET 10.4. DEVELOPING AND IMPLEMENTING STRATEGIES FOR ACHIEVING YOUR DESIRED POSITION (CONTINUED).

Column 1 Determining Your Strategies (Enter your response to the statement below in Column 2.)	Column 2 Response to statement in Column 1 (check one)			Column 3 Plan for Developing and Implementing the Strategy (Complete this section if your response to Column 2 is "Somewhat Agree" or "Disagree")			
	Agree	Somewhat Agree	Disagree	Activities (Example activities are in italics.)	Respon-sible Persons Examples	Resources Needed Examples	Time-frame
Media relations: We get frequent, positive media coverage from our target media.				We want to focus on getting posi-tive media coverage now. We will (list activities) • *Issue press releases* • *Hold press conferences*	*Commu-nications coordina-tor*	*Board and executive spokesper-sons, staff time and expertise*	
Special campaign (for example, for major changes): We are prepared to initiate a special media campaign to announce a major change or recent accomplishment.				We want to initiate a special cam-paign now. We will (list activities) • *Prepare our message* • *Train internal stakeholders* • *Issue press release* • *Hold press conference* • *and so on*	*Commu-nications coordina-tor*	*Board and executive spokesper-sons, staff time and expertise*	
Community relations: We are able to reach out directly to the public with our message.				We want to communicate with the community now. We will (list activities) • *Have a booth at the fair* • *Send a van around the community* • *Host a community event*	*Commu-nications coordina-tor*	*Board and executive spokesper-sons, staff time and expertise*	

Play to Win by David La Piana, ISBN 0-7879-6813-7, cloth, copyright © 2005 Jossey-Bass, An Imprint of Wiley.

public. Then complete the rest of the table for each strategy you select. By doing so, you will create the outline of a simple plan for developing and implementing the strategy.

Assessing Your Outcomes

Just as you assessed the outcomes of your strategies for cultivating relationships with third-party payers and attaining your desired levels of funding (Chapter Eight) and for those related to your efforts to retain the best human resources (Chapter Nine), you need to assess the outcomes of your strategies related to the media and public awareness. Establish specific objectives and periodically assess your performance against them. Set timeframes for reviewing your achievements. At these points, compare your actual outcomes to your targets. If you do not achieve your targets, determine what changes you need to make and keep working at it.

CONCLUSION: AWAKENING TO COMPETITIVE STRATEGY

The nonprofit sector is awakening to the potential and possibilities offered by competitive strategy. I have attempted to place this awakening within both economic and psychological contexts to help you to see the dynamics that both push nonprofits toward and repel them away from more openly embracing competitiveness. But what of those underlying dynamics themselves, and the future of competition in the sector?

- Will competitiveness become a regular topic for open consideration among nonprofit leaders? For example, will it be featured on conference agendas and be the subject of books and articles as often as collaboration?
- Will third-party payers take a more balanced view—with both collaboration and competition acknowledged and supported as legitimate strategies for their grantees?
- Will nonprofit leaders embrace some of the more aggressive competitive aims and strategies, and if so, what effect will it have on the culture of the sector?

These are just a few of the issues that will unfold over the next decade as nonprofits struggle to succeed in increasingly competitive circumstances. One thing is certain: as the number of nonprofits steadily increases and continues to outpace the growth in available resources of all kinds, competition for those resources will become ever more heated. So the question is not really whether you will face increased competition in the future (you certainly will) but how you and other nonprofit leaders will respond and with what impact for the sector?

I am no futurist, and the failures of strategic planning have demonstrated the difficulty inherent in predicting even short-term futures for individual organizations, let alone a longer-term future for an entire sector. The best I can do is to suggest possible directions for some of these issues to unfold, based on my own experience and reading of the sector.

The Future of Competitiveness

First, the dynamics that create competition for resources, as I suggest above, are only going to urge still greater competitiveness over the next decade and beyond. As a result, some nonprofits—those that are able to find a winning combination of mission, governance, leadership, strategy, programs and infrastructure—are going to attract disproportionate pieces of the resource pie, at the expense of nonprofits that continue to struggle with any of these key elements of success. This will occur because third-party payers, particularly private foundations but also, sporadically, local governments, are on a path to becoming more sophisticated sponsors of nonprofit activities. Their burgeoning interest in areas such as outcome measurement and knowledge management will begin to yield metrics for determining which nonprofits are relatively more successful and which are less so. Armed with better information and a concomitant need to be clearer about the outcomes they seek as funders, third-party payers will necessarily become better able to distinguish successful nonprofits from those that are making a good effort but have less to show for it.

This increased third-party payer discernment will take place against a background wherein the traditional nonprofit cultural values of inclusivity and collaboration will remain strong. I am confident that this feature of the environment will not change, since nonprofit leaders are, as a group, intrinsically motivated people who seek social change. Their affinity for others engaged in similar work will remain a powerful driver of the collaborative mind-set.

Moreover, the traditional hesitancy of private foundations to generate controversy or to pass judgment on grantseekers by clearly and publicly choosing some groups over others for a long-term commitment will be at war with the mandates of their newfound metrics, which will allow them to make such distinctions with greater confidence. This means that third-party payer initiatives will emphasize competitiveness with increasing frequency, although some will continue to focus on collaboration.

For example, one foundation recently initiated a competitive awards program for nonprofits in its community, using a head-to-head competitive process adapted from the venture capital world. Ultimately, it chose a first-year cohort of seven non-profits from among more than seventy applicants, bestowing on the winners both substantial long-term operating support and consulting assistance for infrastructure development. At the same time—through a partnership—two other major foundations chose geographic target areas for joint grantmaking, handpicked several nonprofits from different fields and outlooks within each selected community, and initially offered them grants to encourage collaboration on the foundations' agenda.

These two approaches, one highly competitive and the other encouraging collaboration through traditional means, will increasingly coexist as contrasting approaches. Some funders will embrace overt competition in an effort to find grantees for high-leverage investments, while others will continue to choose collaboration, hoping for synergies from the efforts of different nonprofits working closely together.

What about competitiveness itself? Will it truly come out of the closet? Ten years from now, will the concept be no more charged among nonprofit leaders than it currently is among business leaders? I think the answer to that question will vary from subsector to subsector and from community to community. We have seen in the health care field over the past twenty years that the advent of competition from for-profit health care corporations has forced nonprofit hospitals and other providers to either convert to for-profit status or engage in competitive practices that make them virtually indistinguishable from their for-profit competitors. As businesses encroach on other traditionally nonprofit-dominated subsectors, it seems clear that the results will be predictably similar.

For example, the entrance of for-profits into human services fields long dominated by nonprofits has forced nonprofits that wish to survive to become more overtly competitive: to assess their disadvantages relative to the for-profits and move to shore up their hold on the market. They are investing in marketing, improved facilities, new information systems, and other features that allow them to go head to head with larger, better-capitalized corporations. They are also merging or forming alliances with other nonprofits to streamline billing, improve branding, and otherwise protect their markets.

Will nonprofits ever embrace what Houstle (2003) referred to as "the predatory mind-set required for free-market, 'winner-take-all' competition"? In other words, will what I have called exclusive strategies that are intended to drive others from the market or other similarly aggressive steps ever be socially and ethically acceptable to nonprofit leaders? For most, I honestly do not think they will, at least not in the foreseeable future.

While the majority of nonprofit leaders is probably not going to embrace open competition unless led to it by third-party funders sanctioning competitive strategy, aggressive competition is already accepted by a far smaller but influential group of quite successful nonprofit leaders. Those I have spoken with are aware of the benefits of competitiveness, and many are frustrated with the limitations of collaboration. Nonetheless, they feel it is necessary to keep their most aggressive competitive strategies covert. While they see the important role of competition among nonprofits in enhancing the mission-related outcomes the sector seeks, they are intimidated by the prospect of openly espousing these beliefs, because they run so counter to the dominant nonprofit culture. These nonprofit leaders want to avoid being labeled "predatory," as in Houstle's article.

The future of competitive strategy in the sector will also be determined in part by the amount of effort that goes into researching, promoting, and teaching it. As I write this in 2004, the proportion of the nonprofit sector's collective research and development effort that is devoted to this issue is minuscule, especially in comparison to the efforts related to nonprofit collaboration; and it is certainly vastly less than the attention that the business sector devotes to the same topic. This imbalance is unlikely to change until the nonprofit sector's ambivalence about competition itself is resolved; today, competition is both an unacknowledged necessity and a concept that many find foreign, even repugnant.

It is essential that the challenges attendant on competitive strategy in a prosocial environment be aired, discussed and debated. Ultimately, we need a framework for nonprofit competitive strategy that emphasizes, borrowing Paul Light's term, its *nonprofit-like-ness*. Competitiveness is not an area of business strategy that can simply be grafted onto the nonprofit enterprise; rather, nonprofit competitive strategy is a uniquely nonprofit phenomenon. Although it has much in common with business strategy, it is in its essence different, for all the reasons (market failure, third-party payers, psychological and value factors) outlined in this book.

What You Can Do

Given what you have read, what can you do to move the topic of competitiveness farther onto the nonprofit stage? Part Three offered suggestions for competitive strategies that you can consider for your nonprofit, many of which can be pursued while still maintaining an outwardly collaboration-friendly organizational face. Here are five things that you can do in the next twelve months to legitimate your organization's competitiveness:

1. Do not embark on a strategic planning process, which, we know from experience and the research literature (especially Mintzberg, 1994), is likely to result in a set of largely operational goals. Instead, undertake a competitiveness review. Look at the activities you offer and the internal functions that support

them in light of the choices your constituents (customers, third-party payers, staff, board members, and so on) might make. Compare yourself dispassionately with your direct and indirect competitors on key dimensions, and give yourself a grade from A to F in each area. Discuss the results widely within your organization, asking, "Why do (customers, third-party payers, and so on) choose us, and why do they choose Competitor X?" Then ask, "What can we do to enhance their likelihood of choosing us?"

2. Write a paper or give a conference presentation, either describing your nonprofit's experience of competing or discussing your competitive strategy. Share your real-life experiences and lessons. By doing so, you will begin to break down the walls of resistance to airing the concept.

3. The next time someone asks for your input on a conference agenda, tell them you want to hear about nonprofit competitive strategy or how nonprofits can compete in order to advance their missions. Spread the word.

4. Encourage discussion both within and outside of your nonprofit that focuses on the ways that you and other nonprofit leaders attract a wide range of resources, where they come from, and who wins and who loses in the resource competition.

5. Form an ad hoc competitiveness committee or work group within your nonprofit that draws strategic thinkers from all levels of staff and includes board members. Task the group with ensuring that your organization remains competitive—that those choosing to purchase or use a service or activity will prefer yours over others'. Perhaps your group will decide to form a market research team as described in this book and will then engage in the market and competitor research I suggest.

The Last Word

Finally, remember that because you are a nonprofit leader, your own attitudes are a primary driver of change in your organization. If you embrace increased competitiveness, over time there is a good chance that you will motivate a substantial shift in your organization's attitude as well.

Remember, too, that if you succeed in making your nonprofit more aware of its competitive environment and more mindful of developing its competitive strategy, while others in your market do not yet embrace the concept, that in itself is a competitive advantage.

REFERENCES

Bridges, W. *Managing Transitions.* New York: Perseus Books, 1991.

Collins, J. *Good to Great.* New York: HarperBusiness, 2001.

Goodman, T. (ed.). *The Forbes® Book of Business Quotations.* New York: Black Dog and Levanthal Publishers, 1997.

Hall, P. D. "Historical Perspectives on Nonprofit Organizations." In R. Herman and Associates, *The Jossey-Bass Handbook of Nonprofit Leadership and Management.* San Francisco: Jossey-Bass, 1994.

Herman, R., and Associates. *The Jossey-Bass Handbook of Nonprofit Management and Leadership.* San Francisco: Jossey-Bass, 1994.

Hopkins, K., and Hyde, C. "The Human Service Managerial Dilemma: New Expectations, Chronic Challenges and Old Solutions," *Administration in Social Work,* 2002, *26*(3), 1–15.

Houstle, P. "Collaboration, Competition or Cannibalism?" *Association Management,* June 2003, pp. 68–69.

Kearns, K. *Private Sector Strategies for Social Sector Success.* San Francisco: Jossey-Bass, 2000.

Kohm, A., La Piana, D., and Gowdy, H. *Strategic Restructuring; Findings from a Study of Integrations and Alliances Among Nonprofit Social Service and Cultural Organizations in the United States.* Chicago: Chapin Hall Center for Children, University of Chicago, June 2000.

Kouzes, J. M., and Posner, B. Z. *The Leadership Challenge.* (3rd ed.) San Francisco: Jossey-Bass, 2002.

La Piana, D. *The Nonprofit Mergers Workbook.* St. Paul, Minn.: Amherst H. Wilder Foundation, 2000.

La Piana, D. "Real Collaboration: A Guide for Grantmakers," 2001. Online at http://www.lapiana.org/consulting/research/written.html.

Light, P. "The Content of Their Character: The State of the Nonprofit Workforce." *Nonprofit Quarterly,* Fall 2002a, pp. 6–16.

Light, P. *Pathways to Nonprofit Excellence*. Washington, D.C.: Brookings Institution, 2002b.

MacMillan, I. C. "Competitive Strategies for Not-for-Profit Agencies." In R. Lamb (ed.), *Advances in Strategic Management*, Vol. 1. Greenwich, Conn.: JAI Press, 1983.

Mattessich, P., Murray-Close, M., and Monsey, B. *Collaboration: What Makes it Work*. (2nd ed.) St. Paul, Minn.: Amherst H. Wilder Foundation, 2001.

McCambridge, R., and Salamon, L. M. "In but Not of the Market." *Nonprofit Quarterly*, Spring 2003, pp. 8–14.

Miller, C. "Hidden in Plain Sight: Understanding Nonprofit Capital Structure." *Nonprofit Quarterly*, Spring 2003, pp. 16–22.

Mintzberg, H. *The Rise and Fall of Strategic Planning*. New York: Free Press, 1994.

National Center for Charitable Statistics. *Registered Nonprofit Organizations by State*. [http://nccsdataweb.urban.org/NCCS/Public/index.php]. Apr. 2004.

Nielsen, K. "Collaboration Resource List." Amherst H. Wilder Publishing Center. [www.wilder.org/pubs/collab_bibliography/collaboration_bibliography.htm]. Jan. 2003.

Osborne, D., and Gaebler, T. *Reinventing Government: How the Entrepreneurial Spirit Is Transforming the Public Sector*. New York: Plume, 1993.

Porter, M. E. "What Is Strategy?" *Harvard Business Review*, Nov.–Dec. 1996, pp. 61–78.

Ray, K. *The Nimble Collaboration*. St. Paul, Minn.: Amherst H. Wilder Foundation, 2002.

Salamon, L. M. "The Nonprofit Sector and the Future of the Welfare State." *Nonprofit and Voluntary Sector Quarterly*, 1989, *18*(1), 11–24.

Smith, S. R. "Managing the Challenges of Government Contracts." In Robert Herman and Associates, *The Jossey-Bass Handbook of Nonprofit Leadership and Management*. San Francisco: Jossey-Bass, 1994.

ADDITIONAL RESOURCES

Adams, C., and Perlmutter, F. "Leadership in Hard Times: Are Nonprofits Well-Served?" *Nonprofit and Voluntary Sector Quarterly*, 1995, *24*, 253–262.

Allison, M., and Kaye, J. *Strategic Planning for Nonprofit Organizations.* New York: Wiley, 1997.

Angelica, E. *Crafting Effective Mission and Vision Statements.* St. Paul, Minn.: Amherst H. Wilder Foundation, 2001.

Austin, J. E. *The Collaboration Challenge.* New York: Drucker Foundation, 2000.

Blankenship, A. B., Breen, G. E., and Dutka, A. *State of the Art Marketing Research.* (2nd ed.) Chicago: American Marketing Association and Contemporary Publishing Group, 1998.

Bonk, K., Griggs, H., and Tynes, E. *The Jossey-Bass Guide to Strategic Communications for Nonprofits.* San Francisco: Jossey-Bass, 1998.

Feldman, M. L., and Spratt, M. F. *Five Frogs on a Log.* New York: HarperBusiness, 1999.

Gray, B. *Collaborating.* San Francisco: Jossey-Bass, 1989.

Heifitz, R., and Linsky, M. *Leadership on the Line.* Boston: Harvard Business School Press, 2002.

Herman, R., and Heimovics, R. *Executive Leadership of Nonprofit Organizations.* San Francisco: Jossey-Bass, 1991.

Horwitch, M., and Prahalad, C. K. "Managing Multi-Organization Enterprises: The Emerging Strategic Frontier." *Sloan Management Review*, 1981, *22*(2), 3–16.

INDEPENDENT SECTOR and the Urban Institute. *The New Nonprofit Almanac and Desk Reference.* San Francisco: Jossey-Bass, 2002.

Kaplan, R., and Norton, D. P. *The Strategy-Focused Organization: How Balanced Scorecard Companies Thrive in the New Business Environment.* Boston: Harvard Business School Press, 2001.

Kohm, A., and La Piana, D. *Nonprofit Strategic Restructuring: Mergers, Integrations, and Alliances.* New York: Praeger, 2003.

La Piana, D. *Beyond Collaboration: Strategic Restructuring of Nonprofit Organizations.* (Rev. ed.) Washington, D.C.: James Irvine Foundation and National Center for Nonprofit Boards, 1998.

La Piana Associates. *Supplemental Assessment Tool for Start-Ups.* Washington, D.C.: Grantmakers for Effective Organizations, 2003.

Letts, C. W., Ryan, W. P., and Grossman, A. *High-Performance Nonprofit Organizations: Managing Upstream for Greater Impact.* New York: Wiley, 1999.

Light, P. *Making Nonprofits Work: A Report on the Tides of Nonprofit Management Reform.* Washington, D.C.: Brookings Institution, 2000.

McIlnay, D. P. *How Foundations Work.* San Francisco: Jossey-Bass, 1998.

McKinsey & Company. "Effective Capacity Building in Nonprofit Organizations." Report prepared for Venture Philanthropy Partners. [http://venturephilanthropypartners.org/learning/reports/capacity/capacity.html]. Aug. 2001.

Mintzberg, H., Ahlstand, B., and Lampel, J. *Strategy Safari.* New York: Free Press, 1998.

Mintzberg, H., Lampel, J., Quinn, J. B., and Ghoshal, S. *The Strategy Process: Concepts, Contexts, Cases.* New York: Prentice Hall, 2003.

O'Neill, M. *The Third America: The Emergence of the Nonprofit Sector in the United States.* San Francisco: Jossey-Bass, 1989.

Oster, S. *Strategic Management for Nonprofit Organizations: Theory and Cases.* London: Oxford University Press, 1995.

Porter, M. E. *Competitive Advantage: Creating and Sustaining Superior Performance.* New York: Free Press, 1985.

Rea, L. M., and Parker, R. A. *Designing and Conducting Survey Research: A Comprehensive Guide.* (2nd ed.) San Francisco: Jossey-Bass, 1997.

Salamon, L. *America's Nonprofit Sector.* New York: Foundation Center, 1999.

Schein, E. H. *Organizational Culture and Leadership.* (2nd ed.) San Francisco: Jossey-Bass, 1997.

Senge, P. *The Fifth Discipline.* New York: Doubleday, 1990.

Stern, G. J. *Marketing Workbook for Nonprofit Organizations,* Vol. 1: *Develop the Plan.* (2nd ed.) St. Paul, Minn.: Amherst H. Wilder Foundation, 2001.

Strategic Press Information Network. "The SPIN Tool Kit" [www.spinproject.org/resources/tutorials].

Sull, D. N. "Why Good Companies Go Bad." *Harvard Business Review,* July–Aug. 1999, pp. 1–9.

Van de Ven, A. "On the Nature, Formalization, and Maintenance of Relations Among Organizations." *Academy of Management Review,* 1976, *4,* 24–36.

Weick, K. E., and Sutcliffe, K. M. *Managing the Unexpected.* San Francisco: Jossey-Bass, 2001.

Winer, M., and Ray, K. *The Collaboration Handbook: Creating, Sustaining, and Enjoying the Journey.* St. Paul, Minn.: Amherst H. Wilder Foundation, 1994.

Wolfred, T., Allison, M., and Masaoka, J. *Leadership Lost: A Study on Executive Director Tenure and Experience.* San Francisco: CompassPoint Nonprofit Services, 1999.

INDEX